Elaine Hinnant
Spring 1987 P.T.S.

FINDING HOPE AGAIN

HARPER & ROW, PUBLISHERS

SAN FRANCISCO

Cambridge
Hagerstown
Philadelphia
New York

1817

London
Mexico City
São Paulo
Sydney

Finding Hope Again

A Guide to

Counseling the Depressed

ROY W. FAIRCHILD

To Verna,

whose constant love

has nourished my hope and my faith

FINDING HOPE AGAIN: *A Guide to Counseling the Depressed.* Copyright © 1980 by
Roy W. Fairchild. All rights reserved. Printed in the United States of America. No
part of this book may be used or reproduced in any manner whatsoever without
written permission except in the case of brief quotations embodied in critical arti-
cles and reviews. For information address Harper & Row, Publishers, Inc., 10 East
53rd Street, New York, NY 10022. Published simultaneously in Canada by Fitz-
henry & Whiteside Limited, Toronto.

FIRST HARPER & ROW PAPERBACK EDITION PUBLISHED IN 1985.

Designed by Jim Mennick

Library of Congress Cataloging in Publication Data

Fairchild, Roy W
  FINDING HOPE AGAIN.

  Includes bibliographical references and index.
  1. Pastoral medicine. 2. Depression, Mental.
3. Hope. I. Title.
BV4335.F34   1980   253.5   79-2988
ISBN 0-06-062326-8

85 86 87 88 89   10 9 8 7 6 5 4 3 2 1

Contents

Preface

No counselor today can fail to notice the staggering number of despondent people in his or her community. And no pastors have to look very far to see the faces of depression in their congregations. On a visit to a home, the pastor hears a woman say, "My life has no meaning since Joe's gone . . . What's the use of living?" This is a contemporary echo of what the pastor encounters in study when reading Job, Ecclesiastes, the Psalms, Jeremiah, or the words of St. Paul. Pastors, too, find themselves in periods of discouragement, if not depression, unable to move out of their inertia and apathy. What the psychological disciplines have called *depression* has been known and portrayed through all recorded history. The nomenclature may be as young as psychiatry, but the experience is as old as the race.

I have written this book to help pastors, counselors, and other care-givers to better understand depression and to provide the kind of care which may help to lift the misery of melancholy and to activate hope in the sufferer's life. The National Institute of Mental Health estimates that up to eight million

Americans are suffering severe depressions and need immediate help. If we add to that figure the milder despondency, anguish, and dejection people may feel after a loss or hurt, we
begin to see why depression has been called "the common
cold of mental disorder" in our time. But the encouraging fact
is that depression is among the most responsive of all emo-
tional-mental-spiritual ills when given appropriate pastoral,
psychological, and medical care. In these pages I try to convey
our best understandings of depression, and several hope-evoking strategies, without using the technical jargon intelligible
to only a few.

The viewpoint of this book is that depression is not only a
matter for psychiatry and clinical psychology; it is a major concern of philosophy and theology as well. Norman Cousins,
former editor of *Saturday Review,* confirmed this opinion in a
1979 conference on philosophy, held at Dominican College,
San Rafael, California, when he stated the following as one of
the most important things he had learned in life: "The tragedy
of life is not death, but what dies inside while we are living.
... We must recognize that we get our basic energy not from
turbines but from hope." In a biblical metaphor, depression
can be conceived as a wilderness journey, symbolizing the experience of being lost in a desert place, lonely, without water
flowing, and in great danger from thorns and beasts. But it is
also a place where angels minister, where persons have found
transformation, a new identity, and direction. Depression is a
painful spiritual condition out of which much growth can
come.

We can think of a book as a person's heart in another person's hands. The motivation for my research and writing did
not come out of a merely theoretical interest in the subject.
Through more than thirty years of ministry in church, university, seminary, and clinical settings, I have struggled with the
meanings of depression and have sought ways to relieve it. My
own occasional depressions helped me to know first-hand the
way such misery can immobilize one and lower the flame of
life. Through Jungian psychotherapy, I learned that depression can actually be a friend which can lead one to deeper life

and new values and meaning. In this book, I will share an experience of going through that wilderness.

I am grateful to San Francisco Theological Seminary for granting me the sabbatical leave that made this research and writing possible. Invaluable editorial assistance was provided by my wife, Verna, who also greatly stimulated my thinking through her experience in grief counseling and suicide prevention work. I am deeply indebted to Thelma Furste, our faculty secretary, who typed the manuscript with her characteristic cheerfulness, precision, and care, and for her keen editorial eye. John Shopp of Harper & Row was a helpful source of overall guidance which will, I hope, make this book useful for pastors, counselors, and paraprofessionals. I want to express my gratitude for the encouragement and constructive feedback which has been offered by my friends in the ministry, especially the Rev. Dr. C. James Miller, the Rev. John Najarian, the Rev. Margaret Veneman, and Professor David Willis. My friends and psychiatric consultants, Crittenden E. Brookes, M.D., Ph.D., and William Alex, M.D., have generously shared their knowledge and insights with me. Without the careful reading and reality-testing of my ideas by all these colleagues, the book would lack the accuracy and relevance which it seeks to embody. It is my earnest desire that *Finding Hope Again* will increase the momentum of the reader's own search for creative ways of activating hope with those who are going through the dark night of depression.

1. The Many Faces of Depression

Pastors well-acquainted with their congregations are often puzzled and anxious about the depressed persons within the church. Depression and despair are baffling phenomena, even to present-day health professionals. In an attempt to understand their low moods, many people can identify with Shakespeare's Antonio, who reflected on his condition:

> In sooth, I know not why I am so sad
> It wearies me; you say it wearies you.
> But how I caught it, found it, or came by it,
> What stuff 'tis made of, whereof it is born,
> I am to learn;
> And such a want-wit sadness makes of me
> That I have much ado to know myself.
>
> —Merchant of Venice, I, 1, ll. 1–7

Depression, as a distressing human experience, was known for thousands of years before the bard. It is described in early Egyptian manuscripts, in the Old and New Testaments, and in the writings of the classical Greek physicians. Hippocrates saw melancholia (*melan chole*=black bile) as an anguish of mind accompanied by fear and sadness. Just sixty years ago, a giant step was taken by Sigmund Freud in his classic paper of 1917 "Mourning and Melancholia," in which the new psychoanalytic spotlight was brought to bear on these unwelcome perennial intruders on human peace and equilibrium. Freud, as we shall see, has a useful word for us, but not a last word.

Since Freud's time, the categories of depression have proliferated in the field of psychiatry, and confusion is rampant. A short list would include: neurotic, psychotic, reactive, endogenous, agitated, involutional, acute, chronic, masked, senile, mixed, claiming, manic-depressive, self-blaming, unipolar depressive disorder, bipolar mood disorder, postpartum. In my opinion, specific definitions of all these categories (assuming they are valid) are not necessary for pastoral care, but a pastor does need to understand the different degrees of depression he sees in his people. He also needs a rudimentary understanding of some of the basic dynamics of depression to know how best to activate hopefulness and when and how to collaborate with health professionals. A pastor should be slow to classify a suffering person with a one-word or a one-phrase label from a diagnostic manual, but he needs to be aware of the clinical observations that lie behind these labels. Understanding depressed persons will take all the insight he can gain from every field of endeavor. What Martin Buber says about "truth seekers" is applicable to pastoral theology and the health professions alike:

> The investigator cannot truthfully maintain his relationship to reality—a relationship without which all his work becomes a well-regulated game—if he does not again and again, whenever it is necessary, gaze beyond the limits [of his field] into a sphere which is not his sphere of work, yet which he must contemplate with all his power of research in order to do justice to his task.[1]

Religious Expressions of Depression

The pastor's religious orientation will often throw light upon this particular form of human misery. The Jewish and Christian communities, over the centuries, have had much more experience with depression and despair than is commonly realized. Where can we find more poignant expressions of the downcast spirit than in the third chapter of Job? Job presents a painful picture of *despair*, the feeling that one no longer has sufficient purpose to go on living.

> I wish I had died in my mother's womb
> Or died the moment I was born. . . .
> Why let men go on living in misery?
> Why give light to men in grief?
> They wait for death,
> But it never comes;
> They prefer a grave to any treasure.
> They are not happy until they are dead and buried.
> God keeps their future hidden
> And hems them in on every side.
> Instead of eating, I mourn,
> And can never stop groaning.
> Everything I fear and dread comes true.
> I have no peace, no rest,
> And my troubles never end.
>
> (Job 3:11, 20–26, TEV)

More powerful than any clinical description of depression for many spiritually sensitive people are the words of Psalm 13, as Leslie Brandt translated them:[2]

> O God, sometimes you seem so far away.
> I cannot in this moment sense Your presence
>   or feel your power.
>   The darkness about me is stifling.
> This depression is suffocating.
> How long, O God, do I have to live in this void?
> O God, how long?
>   Break into this black night, O God;
>   fill in this vast emptiness.

> Enter into my conflict
>> lest I fall never to rise again.

And then the internal affirmation that gives the Psalmist hope:

> I continue to trust in Your ever-present love.
> I shall again discover true joy
>> in my relationship to You.
> I will proclaim Your praises, my Lord,
>> for you will never let me go.

In the early Middle Ages, the condition known as *accidie*, common in monastaries, was explored by theologians. Spiritual torpor, deep apathy, and despondency were its symptoms. Among the causes attributed to this condition were hidden anger and an imbalance among the bodily juices. Many modern clinicians have not gone much beyond these early explanations.

Pastoral Situations in the Contemporary Church

In the contemporary church, pastors confront depression in many forms. The following (disguised to hide real identities) are some examples.

JOHN BLACK

The pastor was not too surprised when he received the phone call that John Black was dead. What did shock him was the information from the neighbor who found him that his death was a suicide; John had overdosed on Seconal (sleeping pills). At seventy-six, John was apparently "going down hill," or so his friends in the church said. His hearing was failing. Some wondered out loud about senility. He forgot about meetings, and seemed withdrawn when persuaded to come to the Senior Citizens luncheon. At the luncheon, he ate scarcely anything and seemed morose.

The pastor knew it had been a bad year for John Black. His wife, with whom he had been very close, had died just over a year ago. Although grief-stricken, he seemed lost and stoic at the funeral. In the subsequent weeks, the pastor had called on him several times, as had parish visitors. He was reluctant to see anyone. The house was usually a mess, with dirty dishes piled high in the kitchen and empty cans overflowing the garbage bin. When the pastor came, John seemed willing enough to talk, but mostly about his arthritis and his inability to do anything with his hands (he had been a carpenter most of his life). Though resistant to coming out to church, he did volunteer that he occasionally watched religious programs on television. From what the pastor knew of these programs, they stressed salvation in the life beyond.

A month ago, when he saw John last, the pastor found him arranging picture albums, financial papers, and preparing to give his favorite tools to a neighbor he liked (the one who checked up on him frequently). As the pastor thought back on that visit, it seemed as if John Black was preparing to "close up shop." Why hadn't he seen it then? What might he have done, he wondered. Now he must meet with John's son and his wife who had flown in from another state.

LYNN BAKER

Lynn's mother, an active church officer, phoned the pastor just before Lynn arrived home for the Christmas holidays. Lynn was planning to drop out of college, she said, and hinted at other difficulties. Would the pastor see Lynn tomorrow?

Lynn had been president of the church high school fellowship two years before. A beautiful girl, she had everything going for her, the pastor thought. She had given a remarkable "sermon" a few days before leaving for the university, and many of the congregation were deeply impressed with her spirituality and intellect. Her high school teachers were not surprised at her performance. She had entered the university on a fine scholarship; good grades came easily to her. Her proud parents couldn't do enough for their only child. Boys were eager for her attentions. In the yearbook, everyone said that their head cheerleader had great things to look forward to. One year after entering the university, Lynn had changed.

The pastor hardly recognized Lynn when she slumped into

a chair in his office; her face was glum and haggard. Almost without a greeting for him, whom she had known so well, she spoke of her emptiness and her terrible feeling of sadness. The year was a disaster; her courses were impersonal and boring. The school was overrated. So bad was it that she had cut two classes extensively, received Fs, and lost her scholarship. The pastor inquired whether anything else had made it "a disaster."

After forty minutes of detailing her disappointment with the university, Lynn haltingly confessed that her love life was also a disaster. She had been living with a university drop-out for several months; he had introduced her to sex and "soft" drugs. She had met him at a school rally. Two months later he left her. She felt he was a leech who made her feel dirty and exploited. She was so upset that her menstrual period was off and, thinking herself pregnant, she overdosed on the tranquilizers she had received from the University Health Service when she couldn't sleep. She phoned them just as she felt herself going under. They had rescued her and referred her to a university psychiatrist. After one interview, she decided to pack and leave for home.

Her mother didn't know the whole story, she said. Would the pastor keep it confidential? Her faith didn't mean much to her now; Albert Camus was right about how absurd life is. Still, when asked if she'd like to come back to talk more, she readily agreed. Hoping to reassure her, the pastor reminded her of her former achievements, which she passed off as "kid stuff—I fooled everyone." She thanked the pastor profusely and said he was a lot more helpful than "that psychiatrist."

In subsequent sessions, Lynn appeared to be happier, and dressed in attractive, rather provocative clothes. She wanted to talk and talk and began to phone for extra appointments with the pastor. She had decided not to return to school after Christmas. Perhaps she could help out around the church, she volunteered. As the pastor felt Lynn was beginning to cling, to idealize him, and to demand more and more time, he decided to make an appointment with a mental-health consultant, a friend of his. Something just didn't feel right to him.

ELLEN O'CONNELL

Ellen, a thirty-year-old housewife, a key "mover" in the congregation's young couples club, opened her appointment with tears and complained to the pastor that she just had to drop the office she held in the couples group. She felt her life was falling apart; maybe she was losing her mind. She would have to withdraw from all her responsibilities at church and at her son's school, and she felt terribly guilty about it. Did anything happen recently to make her feel so upset, the pastor asked.

"Just two Sundays ago, when you baptized that baby, I began to cry and couldn't stop." She reported that she had felt down in the dumps for several weeks, and was terribly bothered with insomnia. She found it extremely hard to get up in the morning. Sometimes when Bob left for work, she was still asleep; she felt terrible, she said, for not getting his breakfast. She had no appetite for her own. (The pastor reflected on the crib death of Ellen and Bob's third child, just two years ago, but he did not voice his thoughts to Ellen. Could it be she still hadn't worked through this grief? He wondered. Her vivaciousness and sheer activity around the church had convinced him that she had come through that tragedy rather well.)

"Ellen, you said you felt you would fall apart. What did you think would happen to you?" asked the pastor. Hesitatingly, Ellen said she was afraid she'd have to go back to the hospital where she had had shock therapy five years ago. "You didn't know you had a 'crazy' in your church, did you, pastor?" He replied in a matter-of-fact way that a number of people in the church had had special help from time to time to overcome the stresses in their lives, and that he respected them for knowing when they needed it. "Is it possible that you've come to me just now because you'd like to get help, Ellen?"

Relieved that he had articulated her very wish, she said she would like to find psychiatric help in this community, which was still fairly new to her family. She related that she had been in and out of therapy for years before moving to this town; she had been given lithium, she said, for her high periods. How did her family view her moods, the pastor asked.

"Bob said I drove him crazy for a while. First, I'd be low and worried about everyone, and then I was so active and giddy that I wouldn't stop to eat or sleep. I spent so much I threw our checkbook out of balance several times. Bob was ready to leave me until we began to understand, as the psychiatrist explained it, what this 'manic-depression' business was all about."

The pastor assured her that together they would search for suitable psychiatric help. She should not worry about her duties at the church; they would talk about what she could handle later. He asked Ellen if she would mind if he consulted with the psychiatrist from time to time so he would know how best to help her. She'd welcome that, she said; she needed his counseling so that her faith might overcome her hopelessness. She wondered if she and Bob might not see him together for some conversations. The pastor said he would be glad to see them.

LANGDON ELDRIDGE

Eight months ago, Langdon, a member of the official board of the church, had been selected by the school board to be principal of Emerson High School. Long a favorite among college-bound students as a teacher of literature, he was a scintillating lecturer and turned students on even when they didn't expect to be. Langdon was a perfectionist; he sculpted his writing so carefully and painstakingly that he published very little. But what he did get into print was acknowledged as superior. For years, though, he had felt in a rut. He knew this was probably the midlife plateau he read about in every popular magazine. Yet he wasn't one to break out with adventures or affairs. He was well married, and marriage was the liveliest part of his life. An advancement to principal would bring some new life, he was sure, and the salary he needed to take some of the trips he and his wife had dreamed of.

The pastor and his friends at church showered him with congratulations. Just the kind of man with integrity and imagination we need as principal, he was told. Soon after Langdon's advancement, the pastor found his face more often anxious than joyful as he sat with the official board. He often looked preoccupied, and sometimes very sad. The pastor invited Langdon to drop in and see him, commenting briefly on the constant look of concern and dejection he had noticed.

It didn't take Langdon long to make an appointment with the pastor. When they started talking, he quickly got into the mistake he had made by leaving teaching for administration. It was a clear case, he said, of the Peter Principle, being elevated to the point of one's incompetency. The job was not at all as he pictured it would be. He was trouble shooting constantly; he was a PR man; he was a flunky; he was a target. Sometimes he felt so low, he was virtually nonfunctional. He didn't trust his decisions any more. He procrastinated; the work piled up on his desk in spite of a good secretary. He dreaded meeting the public at PTA meetings and often fantasized getting sick so that he could not attend. He thought about death quite a bit and read the obituary columns more carefully than he used to. Maybe he would drop dead of a heart attack on the job, he mused, that would be one way out.

The pastor listened carefully to Langdon and was impressed with the change that had come over him during the last months. Here was a "successful" man believing he was all washed up, not long after his promotion. He asked Langdon what he missed most from his former life, what he felt he had lost. Tears welled up in Langdon's eyes as he spoke of his teaching and writing, and his time to read. "I picked up Tolstoy's *The Death of Ivan Ilych* the other day and found myself in it. The real agony of death, says Tolstoy, is the final realization that we have not really lived our life, that we did not do what we most dearly desired. That's it, Pastor, in a nutshell." "Are you really trapped, Langdon?" asked the pastor. "Have you really given away all your options? The Gospel affirms we are always free for new life. Why don't we continue to meet together to discuss the possibilities?"

These four pastoral situations contain the ingredients for much of the discussion that follows. We will come back again and again to these four people in our observations on depression. For the moment, let us look at what they have in common.

First, *change*—in thinking, feeling, and acting. Whether it has come on gradually or suddenly, the depressed person shows a contrast in what he is now compared with his usual self. John Black has become more reclusive and less social. Lynn Baker is almost the opposite of her predepressed self in her lack of achievement, her moral conduct, and her withdrawal from a normally active social life. Ellen O'Connell atypically wants to drop her responsibilities and shows an extreme fluctuation in mood and activity. And Langdon Eldridge changes from the competent, self-assured teacher to the fearful, angry, and disillusioned administrator, hopeless about his future. Change is one of the first signs the care-giver might notice as he lives and works with people.

Secondly, *loss* is apparent in all of these people's lives. Depression almost always involves a loss of some kind. Our examples range from the concrete losses of John Black's beloved wife and his physical agility and of Ellen O'Connell's baby, to the less tangible but nonetheless powerful loss of work satisfaction, security, and aspirations for Langdon Eldridge, and of the ideal public image and effortless successes, as well as of religious faith, for Lynn Baker.

Third, the most obvious sign of depression in each of these parishioners is their *sad mood*, varying, of course, in intensity, in pain, and in sense of hopelessness. Pastors confront this mood in everyday conversation: "Nothing I do turns out right." "Without him, my life is not worth living." This kind of comment is a warning flag.

The Feminine Face of Depression

Even though the pastoral situations just presented featured an equal number of men and women, it is a well-established fact that, in industrialized Western countries, more women than men experience depression. In the United States anywhere from two to five times as many women as men are likely to be diagnosed as "depressed." In a recent article summarizing the research, "The More Sorrowful Sex,"[3] Maggie Scarf discards the too-easy conclusions that these lopsided figures are a product of a poor interpretation of statistics or of galloping female hormones or of the greater number of women who seek help from mental-health professionals. The most competent studies conclude that *many more women than men really are depressed,* regardless of who does or doesn't go to the doctor. Myrna Weissman, director of the Yale University Depression Unit and an epidemiologist by training, completed a community study of representative samples of women in the Northeast and concluded that the number of women interviewed who were depressed (women not in treatment) far exceeded that of men. The number of younger women who have attempted suicide, most of them depressed, has surged upward dramatically in the last ten years.

If women are in fact the more sorrowful sex, why is this so? Several hypotheses have been advanced, some of which will be developed in the next chapter. First, being female in a Western industrialized culture has meant learning to be helpless. Being female often means never being encouraged to become a self-sufficient person. Researcher Martin E. Seligman has substantial evidence linking a sense of "learned helplessness" to depression.[4]

Secondly, women and girls in our society are frequently taught to lower their personal aspirations and to depend upon a dominant male for their well-being. The loss of such a relationship leaves the woman helpless economically and batters her self-esteem. When the pattern of living for the sake of the dominant other and of gaining approval and gratification from that one important person is lost or broken, the result is often depression.

A third reason women more frequently get the blues is suggested by sociologist Jessie Bernard. Though she doesn't minimize the handicapping effects of powerlessness, overdependency, and learned helplessness as causes of malaise, she urges us to look at other crucial changes in women's lives that have been slighted by the psychological theorists. Because the increase in female depression (especially among young women) has coincided with the women's liberation movement, traditionalists are all too ready to see that movement as the primary cause of such depression. Bernard sees the connection going in the opposite direction.[5] She reviews the research supporting the theory that marriage has a protective, supportive effect on males but a detrimental (and often depressive) effect on women.

What is it about modern marriage that contributes to female depression? Bernard's conclusions are two. First, several studies agree that a large group of husbands (about one-third of a representative sample) respond to their wives' low moods and problems by criticizing, rejecting, passive listening, or dismissing them as unimportant. The kind of marital interaction so helpful in working through dejected feelings is not possible for the women married to these particular men. Secondly, modern marriage, so often characterized by high geographical mobility and women's increasing participation in the labor force, has cut off the average woman from women friends she can trust and with whom she can share deeply. It was not always so. In the nineteenth century, Bernard points out, the biological realities of frequent pregnancies, childbirth at home, nursing, and menopause bound women together in physical and emotional intimacy, in a stable community, and formed a distinctive female world of sharing. Such genuine "female homosociality" has decreased markedly in recent decades. Furthermore, the woman-to-woman bonds have been replaced in Western culture by an emphasis on man-woman relationships. It is Bernard's hope that in the sisterhood of the women's movement, a new affiliative style for women might emerge that will fulfill the needs met by the older friendship networks.

The Near-Relatives of Depression

Sadness, sorrow, and dejection, by themselves, are not equivalent to depression as it is clinically understood. Normal *sadness* occurs as a result of unpleasant events which have occurred in a person's life. And, surprisingly, some depressive-states are *not* manifested primarily in low moods. Some forms of "masked" or hidden depression are expressed in overconcern with the body and physical symptoms (mostly in the elderly). A large proportion of older adults classified as "senile" are really depressed. In children and youth, behavior as varied as physical disorders, vandalism, sexual promiscuity, and reclusiveness may have their beginnings in depression. Attraction to rigidly structured cults and totalitarian movements is recognized now as often having roots in depression; the self is seen as helpless unless fortified by a powerful leader. In the middle years, depression is often masked by the excessive use of alcohol and drugs, which temporarily anesthetize the awareness of despondency. The incidence of hidden depression in the modern world is truly staggering.

Depression is not to be equated with *grief*, although inadequate resolution of grief can bring on depression. Grief in adults is distinguishable from depression and has identifiable stages of its own (see the reading list). In children, however, the pathology of grief reactions is often identical to that of depression. Because children gain their selfhood from identification with those they love—their parents and friends—about the most terrible thing that can happen to a child is the death of a loved parent. Many children feel as if their world has come to an end; they have no "self" left. Their world may become unreal to them. A child said to me once in a play therapy session, following the death of her father, "It must be a nightmare. Can you wake me up?"

Anger over being abandoned may pervade the child's life long after the death—even the death of a beloved pet—but children cannot easily label their feelings. Guilt over disobedience or having wished the parent dead does not fade away easily. It used to be thought that children did not get depressed because they did not show the usual signs of depression seen in adults. Depressed children may not cry; they may become withdrawn and fearful. They might run away, even from the surviving parent. They may stop eating. Or the opposite might happen; they become violent or overactive, breaking things because they are so "broken up" inside themselves.

Psychoanalyst René Spitz's studies of institutionalized children who become physically debilitated and irresponsive are studies in childhood depression. Much school absenteeism and fear may be depressive as well as an expression of separation anxiety.

Adults, in their bereavement, may not notice the depression of a child at the very time the child most needs the reassurance and comfort. When grief is not recognized and worked through, a child may go through most of adult life with a pervasive sense of sadness and vulnerability to later losses. The congregation that really cares for its children will be alert to their grief and depression, even though it is masked in many ways. Eda LeShan's book *Learning to Say Goodbye*[6] is a fine resource for such ministry.

Freud distinguished between mourning (grief) and melancholia (depression) in adolescents and adults by noting that in grief the world becomes poor and empty for the griever, whereas in depression it is the ego itself that becomes poor and empty. In depression, as we shall see, it is self-esteem, one's opinion of oneself, which is lowered or lost. Lowered self-esteem is often manifested in feelings of incompetence, helplessness, and lack of resources, of no paths open for change. The temporary dejection of grief is qualitatively different from depression with its prolonged effect on moods, motor behavior, physiological maintenance functions, thought processes, and self-image.

Anxiety and depression are frequently bedfellows, and when they are found together, the condition known as "anxiety depression" results. But anxiety is not the same as depression. Either can predominate the other in a particular person. When we face a loss or threat to our self-esteem, we respond with anxiety and apprehension if we are uncertain about the outcome in the future. But if we become convinced (believing that the threat is inescapable or the loss irretrievable and that this will damage our life), depression replaces anxiety. In depression there is a sense of helplessness; in anxiety, there is fearful uncertainty. In anxiety we do not believe that action is futile and that all doors are shut. We can use the term *despair* for that extreme form of depression in which there is an utter lack of hope; anxiety is seldom linked with despair.

Boredom is a close relative of depression. There isn't much pain in boredom, just apathy and emptiness. The routines of life become drudgery. *Ennui* and weariness transform the world into a wasteland of tedious striving. The bored person often feels a need for stimulation, a craving for excitement; there is not enough to do. Paradoxically, however, the person may feel overwhelmed with too much to do, but what must be done seems meaningless.

With rare exceptions, every life includes some boredom as part of the normal rhythm of active outgoing interest alternating with a routine, passive rest from effort. The inner motor is shut down and we depend on stimulation from the outside, from television or a movie, for example, which moves us into a world of excitement or adventure effortlessly. It is only when boredom becomes the chronic state and the energies of life are withdrawn from action for long periods that we must be concerned. Such boredom is usually an expression of the paralysis that comes from inner conflict, robbing life of meaningful action. In such boredom, the seeds of depression grow.

Depression Is a Family of Symptoms

From what I have said already, it can be seen that depression is a complex phenomenon, with many ingredients. *Clinical depression refers to the slowing down of the whole organism*—emotional, intellectual, and physical—and not to mood alone. A person who becomes depressed may experience changes in a number of ways:

- change in appetite and eating habits
- insomnia or sleeping too much
- low energy level or constant tiredness or boredom
- feelings of inadequacy or guilt
- decreased effectiveness at school, work, or home
- decreased ability to pay attention, or to concentrate and think clearly

- social withdrawal from groups and friends
- loss of interest in and enjoyment of sex
- restriction of involvement in pleasurable activities
- physical and mental slowing down ("psychomotor retardation")
- irritability
- less talkativeness than usual
- pessimistic attitude toward the future
- tearfulness or crying; sad facial expression
- recurrent thoughts of death or suicide
- loss of interest and motivation in activities formerly considered important

The pastor or care-giver should try to be aware of the many facets of an individual's life in which such changes are apparent.

We can now see that in the four pastoral situations presented earlier, each depressed person manifested disturbances in several of these areas. What makes depression so resistant to self-help is the frequent interconnection of physical reactions and mental-emotional responses, which reinforce each other. Tiredness makes the person aware that something is wrong, and this worry increases depression, and so on in a vicious circle. A restraint on muscular activity that is produced by a loss of motivation causes the system to become sluggish and bogged down, and a downhill spiral is in operation. A person who is *disheartened* will regain hope when the situation changes, and a person who is *dejected* will spring up again when there is the prospect of pleasure. But the *depressed* person usually remains stuck in misery, unable to respond to normal encouragement and a change of environment because of impaired self-esteem and the circular process described above. In a very perceptive insight, the author of Proverbs noted the contrast:

> A man's spirit will endure sickness;
> but a broken spirit who can bear?
> (Proverbs 18:14, RSV)

As long as our self-esteem is intact, we have the ability to bear many infirmities and losses, but when our self-esteem is shattered, we give up hope.

The cost in human creativity of such melancholy is high, and the religious community should be concerned with whatever may stand in the way of the human being using his or her full potential for good. Depression has tipped personal and even national and international events one way rather than another. As psychiatrist Nathan Kline notes,

> Because of depression, favorable enterprises have been abandoned because the owner had forebodings of disaster. Important research has been neglected because the investigator imagined difficulties which were not there. Defeat has been snatched from the jaws of victory because a military commander countermanded a campaign which in reality had already succeeded. At a more mundane level, the housewife is too tired to maintain pride in herself or her home; the bright young man with high potential lacks the drive to convert his assets into successful accomplishments.[7]

The waste of gifts and talents should be enough to strengthen our desire to understand the enigma of depression and despair.

2. *In Search of Causes*

In asking what causes depression and despair, we approach an incredibly complicated question, one which has been researched intensively during the last decade. It is not possible here to represent adequately all the theories and supporting research that are available.[1] I will focus on several of the factors in the causation of depression that are most strongly supported in the dominant theories. Later chapters will deal with proposed pastoral strategies for dealing with these factors.

Theories of causation are often divided between those which emphasize psychosocial factors and those which regard these influences as secondary to biochemical imbalance in the organism. Few cases of depression are a matter of either/or, and the pastor, with his Judeo-Christian background, should never forget the body-mind-spirit unity that is presupposed by the scriptures. If the pastor is motivated to read further in these theories, he should know that strong disagreements (indeed, "denominations") exist within the helping professions as to which contributing factors to emphasize in diagnosis and treatment. In a recent book, psychiatrist Jules Bemporad observes:

> It is unfortunate that the study of mental illness has become split into warring camps of organically and psychologically oriented practitioners. Obviously, the clinician cannot ignore the fact that there are biological events occurring in the brain of the patient any more than the chemical researcher can ignore that the substances he is studying are affected by the life experience of the organism.[2]

However, the pastor ought to note carefully as he reads in this area that, with rare exceptions, each school *does* often ignore or minimize the contribution of the other.

The Experience of Loss

Loss is the most consistent theme in the study of depression. Failure at work and school, rejection, death of a loved one, physical disability, marital conflict, financial difficulty, being severed from a familiar role, are common "triggers" for depression. Those losses which cut us off from survival and physical well-being, from the acceptance of those we love, from the roles in which we can feel self-respect and can perform with dignity, and from a comprehensive frame of meaning and values for life, inevitably produce a crisis and, in some people, a depression. Where a person has an inordinate attachment to another person or to a cherished goal, such severance may mean the loss of life's meaning.

Even success can mean a loss, as we saw in the case of Langdon Eldridge (Chapter 1). His loss of cherished functions, the fear of failure and of independence, and his perfectionism contributed to Langdon's depression. In others who have reached goals for which they had struggled long and hard, there is often what Nietzsche described as "the melancholia of everything completed"—it was the striving itself which made life meaningful. The fact that goals reached seldom deliver all the satisfactions that have been anticipated is additional cause for disillusionment. In many religious people, when the success has come as the result of stiff competition, severe guilt feelings sometimes occur; in war, when a friend is killed, this reaction is called *survivor guilt*. Success can lead to despondency, and when all the world expects us to be happy, we may feel guilty for not being happy. Few people in the church understand "success depression," and almost no one offers support to one caught in this miserable condition.

Unexpected loss or change is a powerful trigger for depression. A sudden loss, severing us from familiar sources of support and comfort, can severely disrupt a life, robbing it of meaning. The shock of a sudden death of a family member may leave us without the emotional resources to meet the crisis. In contrast, a gradual loss, though painful, can be prepared for to some extent. Parents can absorb the loss of their last child leaving home, loss brought about by a move to a new city, or some developing physical disability by anticipating how this will change their lives and by gathering their resources for the new step. However, with a sudden diagnosis of terminal illness, for example, the initial impact and recoil is qualitatively different, and often devastating.

Recently, we have become more aware of the depression that comes with the transitions in adult life, when we change our roles and experience a challenge to the assumptions upon which we have so far based our lives. Psychiatrist Roger Gould's book *Transformations*[3] brilliantly documents the shattering of assumptions that reverberate through our being as profound loss at each stage of adult life. In the thirties, he holds, a new way of seeing the world is forced upon us. No longer can a person live by the assumption: "I will do what I am supposed to do and my dreams will come true." Magic hopes are seriously diminished, and with their loss a new view of life must be developed. Likewise, the losses in later midlife have a profound impact: the loss of youth and of youthful dreams and aspirations, the necessity of facing up to our death, and the loss of physical and sexual energies, to mention the most obvious. One investigator of the midlife crisis, Eliot Jaques, sees the forties and fifties as essentially a period of mourning, disappointment, and anger about our inevitable death.[4] Shedding the early assumptions and false hopes upon which we build life is, in the last analysis, a profoundly religious experience; pursuing it can lead to either a new and vital identity or a deadening depression.

The loss of faith and a sense of being abandoned by God is frequently an accompaniment or a cause of depression, as we observed in the words of Job, in Psalm 13, and in the case of Lynn Baker (Chapter 1). Radical doubt is probably always connected with the disappointments and frustrations of life, but the loss of faith is important in its own right. The disillusionments that come when virtue fails to be rewarded, when loved ones die and tragedies befall us in spite of earnest prayer, when the dark nights of the soul proclaim the absence of any God that cares, all bring an emptiness where formerly there was meaning. And for the intellectually inclined person, such as Lynn Baker, the writings of Dostoevsky, Tolstoy, Camus, and Kafka often serve as vehicles to articulate the meaninglessness of life. In our day, the loss of religious experience is seldom shared because *the depth of the religious need cannot be admitted.* It is repressed, as was sex seventy-five years ago. The pastor has an opportunity to explore this often unacknowledged source of depression—the failure to find a spiritual meaning for life.

Humanists, too, lose faith in humanity. In a remarkable record of a disillusioned idealist, the book *Dear Deedee*[5] reveals in diary format the struggles of Dori Schaffer, who finally committed suicide after a growing depression. Dori, a beauty queen, a prize-winning artist, a writer, a Phi Beta Kappa scholar, a Woodrow Wilson fellow, and a promising doctoral candidate, was the only child in a Jewish professional family. She grew up with high aspirations, romanticizing life and believing the world was full of happiness and love. In the 1960s, through a variety of bitter experiences, she became aware of the reality of evil in the world and in all of her relationships:

> Personal friends steal from you, jungles of corporations may practice white collar frauds, and government is too big to touch the lives of people. . . . I will not be disenchanted or hurt any more.

... Death is a sort of utopia, a calm, a quietness. ... If a caring man like John F. Kennedy could be assassinated, what have we really? [p. 221].

Just before killing herself at age twenty-five by an overdose of Nembutal, Dori wrote in the diary she had maintained from the age of fifteen:

I compare myself to Ivan [in *The Death of Ivan Ilych*] where he is being tormented by the feeling that his life was not worthwhile: His mental sufferings were due to the fact that at night, as he looked at Gersim's sleepy, good-natured face with its prominent cheekbones, the question suddenly occurred to him: WHAT IF MY WHOLE LIFE HAS REALLY BEEN WRONG? ... What actions will lead to a satisfying life. ... *What is worth seeking?* [pp. 189–190].

This may be the main question a depressed person seeks to answer when approaching the pastor for help. It is also the question the pastor should raise in counseling if it is not brought up by the depressed person.

Diagnostically, when depression is related to an experience of loss (sometimes not seen at first by the suffering person), it is termed *reactive*. A contrasting category, *endogenous* depression (meaning arising from within), is thought to have no external provoking cause. Metabolic disturbances are often assumed to be primary. However, the triggering cause may not always be obvious; an apparently insignificant event can symbolize and trigger a deeper sense of loss. A continuum may be imagined, moving from a depressed condition where few external precipitating factors prevail to a condition where external losses seem to be crucial. Everything being equal, the probability of recovery from depression is better when external factors play the larger role.

Inadequate Sorrow Work

Loss, though a major factor in the onset of depression, cannot be its sole cause. No situation or loss affects two people alike. And the same person may react differently to similar events at different times. What makes a person vulnerable to depression?

One intriguing lead, especially important for pastors to consider, is discussed by psychiatrists Silvano Arieti and Jules Bemporad in their important book *Severe and Mild Depressions.* Unlike many psychiatrists who see sadness after loss and clinical depression as unrelated phenomena, Arieti sees them on a continuum: *Depression is an unresolved state of sadness and sorrow.* The depressed person is often one who has not adequately worked through a loss in the past. The sorrow remains unprocessed; grief work, with all of its conscious suffering, has not been done. For a variety of reasons, true mourning is bypassed. Conscious suffering, with its confusion and anger, cannot be tolerated at the time the loss takes place, and the sorrow remains within until some point in life when it is evoked again, perhaps by another symbolic loss or one of the major transitions of adult life. In the case of Ellen O'Connell, the crib death of her baby had been immediately followed by compulsive activity in the church, which helped her to avoid the grieving and sorrow work she needed to do. ("Do something useful and you won't brood about it," a friend had advised.) Inadequate sorrow work later erupted into a deep depression when Ellen's memories were evoked again as she witnessed a baby being baptized. Like many people who have delayed their sorrow work, she could not, at first, identify the loss which caused the original sadness.

The beloved wife of a pastor died after a lengthy and painful illness. The week after the funeral he threw himself into his work again with energy and dedication. His people commented on how well he was bearing up and witnessing to his faith. Three months later he "broke down" in a deep depression and required over a year of psychiatric therapy to regain his health and perspective again.

If the grief process is understood, a pastor or knowledgeable friend is in a strategic position to help a person who has sustained a loss to anticipate the phases of grief he can expect to experience. Lynn Caine, author of the eloquent and candid book *Widow*, tells of the importance of knowing what grief entails:

> If only someone who I respected had sat me down after Martin died and said, "Now Lynn, bereavement is a wound. It's like being very, very badly hurt. But you are healthy, you are strong, you will recover. But recovery will be slow. You will grieve and that will be painful. And your grief will have many stages, but all of them will be healing. Little by little, you will be whole again. . . . " There is no avoiding the natural progression of grief—nor should one want to. In this country . . . we tend to forget that happiness has its price and that love must be paid for. . . . I am convinced that if I had known the facts of grief before I had to experience them, it would not have made my grief less intense, not have lessened my misery, minimized my loss or quieted my anger. . . . But it would have allowed me hope. It would have given me courage. I would have known that once my grief was workèd through, I would be joyful again.[6]

Arieti comments that those who do inadequate sorrow work will "remain forever, excessively vulnerable to the disappointments and losses which, for better or worse, form part of human destiny" (p. 184). When a loss occurs, it hurts; it *should* hurt. Those who have studied the effect of delayed grief would agree that blessed are they who mourn, for they shall more quickly find comfort. C.G. Jung long ago concluded that the inability to face and work through normal suffering was a cause of neurosis. In contrast to an American assumption, he says, "suffering is not an illness, but a normal counterpole to happiness. . . . Neurosis is a substitute for legitimate suffering."[7]

Why a person is unable to embrace and work through suffering (to "take up the cross daily") is puzzling. Arieti points to one suspicious characteristic that most depression-prone individuals seem to possess: *they have learned to depend on some external person or goal to constantly reassure them that they are of value.* Without that "dominant other" or "dominant goal," the dejected person experiences the self as empty, abandoned, meaningless, and unnecessary. The loss is often translated into self-accusation and guilt: "If I hadn't done thus and so, she would still be here." Self-esteem is shattered with the loss, and the person seems to be incapable of going through the wrenching process of sorrow work without special help.

Negative Internal Conversations

New understandings from research in cognitive psychology have focused attention on how the depressed person interprets the loss and on the statements that people make to themselves about themselves and their situation. In other words, our internal conversations—how we think and believe—assume a major role in despondency. Depressed people harbor continuous or intermittent negative thoughts about themselves and their futures. *With each negative dialogue, the depressed feeling and the apathy increase.* Many of these internal conversations are so quick, elusive, and automatic that we scarcely know they have been going on. The main point is that there is a conscious thought or idea which almost always intervenes between the external event (or loss) and one's emotional response to it. A young man flunks out of college or joins a cult. His father may react to this event by saying to himself, "I have failed as a parent," and a depressed and guilty mood sets in.

Often these statements to the self are misconceptions, but the depressed person may cling to them. In severe depression and despair, a person continues to engage in negative internal conversations with some of the following themes:

- I am, and will remain, helpless;
- I am losing my mind;
- I alone am responsible for my present condition—I am not angry at anyone;
- I am lonely and rejected by others because I am worthless;
- Things won't ever work out for me.

Cognitive therapists such as Aaron Beck, Victor Raimy, and Albert Ellis[8] focus on what the person is telling himself, often without being aware of it, and the "irrationality" of the statements. Because these thoughts are so automatic, the therapist helps the individual to track these ideas, images, or beliefs; to critically evaluate them; and to talk back to them, as it were.

If a person thinks about a recent event that has upset or depressed him, it should be possible, given the proper help, to sort out three aspects:

1. The event itself;
2. His thoughts, interpretation, and internal conversation about the event;
3. His feelings and response.

Most people are normally aware of only 1 and 3; number 2 slips by their consciousness. To conceive of the mental operations in this way has a distinct advantage for the pastor and the depressed parishioner. People can be led to see that they are not as helpless as they feel. With pastoral or other professional help, they can learn to identify and correct erroneous and one-sided interpretations and beliefs and more adequately assess the possibilities for change. They can explore alternative explanations and engage in active dialogue with the ideas that bring on the depression. When they can be active in their own behalf, helplessness is reduced and, with it, hopelessness.

Particularly helpful is Aaron Beck's "primary triad," in which three major thought patterns in the depressed person are identified.[9] The first component is the *pattern of interpreting events in a negative way.* The person consistently interprets his interactions with the world as representing defeat, deprivation, or disparagement. The person may actually receive ten compliments and one critical comment, but he will focus on the criticism and generalize his thinking: "I always do a lousy job; I won't ever be able to satisfy my teachers."

A second component is a pattern of *viewing himself in a negative way.* Often a comparison with others will bring the thought that others are more attractive, intelligent, or successful, and that he has a physical, mental, or moral defect that will surely result in rejection: "I am a much poorer student than John, and will never get into graduate school."

The third component is the *tendency to view the future in a negative way*, expecting that he will never get over the current distress and that his suffering will continue indefinitely. Hopelessness about ever overcoming current hardships and reaching a goal permeates the thought pattern. The depressed person expects a negative outcome from most every project and undertaking.

In the cognitive school of thought, the negative view more often creates the depressed mood, paralysis of will, passivity, and increased dependency, than vice versa. So if I run into a block in my writing or do not get the response I want from it, I may tell myself that my abilities are deteriorating and there is no future as a writer for me. My depressed mood will not be far behind. I stop going forward in life and go into a depressive hibernation. As my internal conversation changes, my mood may also change. But that change requires much more understanding than simply substituting "positive thinking" for negative thinking.

Pastors must look carefully at this understanding of depression, since belief is clearly paramount and internal conversation ("Why art thou cast down, O my soul?") may be at the heart of the concepts of prayer and religious education. Both prayer and religious education may be means of changing what we learn to say to ourselves about our situation, since in these activities we recognize God as an active participant in our lives. That recognition, manifest too in the internal conversation, does not come easily. Basic beliefs seldom change without a tenacious struggle and hard-earned insight into their roots.

Resentment and Anger Turned Inward

Depressed people seldom show direct hostility to others, but self-reproach and self-hatred are common. So striking was this finding that Sigmund Freud and his followers have made it the basis of the psychoanalytic theory of depression. In the words of Freud,

If one listens patiently to a melancholic's many various self-accu-
sations, one cannot in the end avoid the impression that often the
most violent of them are hardly at all applicable to the patient himself, but that with insignificant modifications they do fit someone
else, someone whom the patient loves or has loved or should
love . . . [10]

Thus Freud emphasized that the depressed person was actually
but unconsciously accusing not himself but rather the disap-
pointing and rejecting "love-object." Disappointment is almost
always due, said Freud, to our exaggerated dependency on a
person who has let us down by abandonment or through
death. A source of a precious supply of love has been lost; the
wish to be taken care of is frustrated. Unable to express anger
toward the loved person, the depressed person turns this anger upon himself and the internalized love object. Freud's theory assumes that if the person is helped to become aware of
the proper target of the anger, and is able to verbalize the
rage, the depression disappears. There is often a burst of relief.

Unacknowledged resentment is frequently a part of the depression the pastor will observe in marital difficulties. For example, one person may resent the deference which the spouse
gives to a mother or father, often neglecting the mate in the
process. But since we may not be able to fault our mate for
generous care of a parent, the anger is repressed and depression ensues. In marriage, emotional and sexual withdrawal
from the mate is a frequent sequel.

We should not assume that misdirected anger does not find
some outlets. Often the depressed person is generally irritable.
"I'm like a sore toe, ready to be stepped on," said one man to
me. The depressed person often punishes the one resented in
subtle and passive ways. "Go away, I am no good for anyone,"
a woman says to her husband, and in her self-isolation and
sulking she is expressing anger at both him and herself. Alien-
ating oneself even more from the loved person by such isolation tactics generally increases the depression and loneliness.
Some investigators point out that many depressed people
make sure that others are affected by their suffering. They may

become demanding and manipulative, getting others to do things for them, forcing loved ones to comply with their wishes, to sympathize, and to sacrifice for them. Since they do not experience a solid sense of self-esteem or personal power to influence the world directly, they try to control it indirectly through their "helplessness." Such continuous claims often evoke a genuine anger or aversion in the others, thus increasing the guilt and isolation of the depressed. A downward spiral has begun.

As I will point out later, pastors may find that depressions caused by inturned anger are very difficult to deal with. The taboo on anger in church circles is deep indeed. The imperative to be "nice" is one of the causes of many breakdowns among Christians.[11]

Freudian theory, however, cannot account for all anger in depression. The pastor should not overlook the fact that *much anger in depressed people is not the cause of depression but a consequence of lowered self-esteem,* deriving from the feeling that one is helpless or hopeless to do anything about one's frustrating situation or loss. Action appears futile. Anger, however, bestows some sense of power or control. The pastor should not assume (with some schools of short-term psychotherapy) that a cathartic expression of the anger, verbally or physically, is all that is needed to help. When anger surfaces, it can be very threatening, both to the person expressing it and to those to whom it is expressed. ("I am afraid I might explode and go to pieces.") Getting in touch with and expressing "bad" feelings does not solve all the problems of a relationship. Filled with guilt and shame, many people go into even deeper despair.

If parishioners can be helped to express their anger close to the time of a loss, much depression might be avoided. If no anger at all is felt at a loss, it is likely that true grief will not be experienced and a healthful mourning will not take place. Theologian-novelist C. S. Lewis revealed this clearly in his personal memoirs, *A Grief Observed.* The death of his wife Joy provoked him to rage, and during a period of his mourning he candidly thought of God as a "cosmic sadist."[12] Stoically refusing to show anger in the grieving process often indicates that one's full humanity is being denied. When the expression of anger is inhibited, the flow of life is restricted and the result may be depression, "a living death."

It is not only the loss of a *person* that provokes normal anger. In his remarkable book *An Elephant's Ballet*, Robert Kemper tells the moving story of how he coped with the loss of sight ordinarily considered essential to his work as a pastor-editor. In his pilgrimage through the trauma of sudden blindness, he takes us from his anxiety, to his anger, to his dejection and loss of self-esteem, and reveals how he worked them through with the help of family and friends. Anger was a part of his grieving.

> I was trying hard to do what I used to do, but I always seemed mad about what I did. . . . I would mouth off, criticize and shout at those islands near mine. Listening to one of my oral tirades over some trivial matter, seven-year old Ginny asked her mother, "Why is Daddy so angry?" . . . Could they not understand that I was angry not because of them or the trivial instance which had brought on the flare-up? Of course they could not . . . because the cause was in me. . . . Inside my head, behind those wounded eyes, an elephant raged. . . . "I'll never make it."[13]

The Experience of Guilt

Closely related to, yet distinct from anger turned inward is the experience of guilt in depression. Some theorists would see the two as identical, but this betrays an inadequate distinction among the several kinds of guilt discussed in this section and the next. Most despondent people do, in fact, communicate a sense of guilt and self-blame during their low periods. Sometimes the guilt seems to be a primary factor in their lowered self-esteem, and sometimes it plays a distinctly secondary role. My impression is that a feeling of guilt is more often seen as associated with their depression by people of middle age and beyond, whereas younger people tend to see the cause of their depressed moods as frustration. Taking elderly people through a "life review"—now a common practice in many therapeutic programs for the aging—often uncovers a sense of guilt and regret about episodes or memories in earlier life over which the person has been obsessively ruminating. The despair encountered in many elderly people can be traced to the realization that there is no opportunity, at this late stage in their lives, to resolve the guilt and to right the balance by restitution or reconciliation. Psychoanalyst Erik Erikson writes eloquently of the disgust and despair that overcome many elderly people when they cannot resolve such "leftovers" and cannot see their lives as having made a meaningful contribution. They need to be reconciled with their past lives. A "healing of the memories" is difficult, but it can be done.[14]

Normal or realistic guilt is very important in the development of every human being. It is the backbone of any responsible society. It helps us become aware when we have hurt others or betrayed our own standards and values. The indispensability of such responsibility is underlined in Karl Menninger's book *Whatever Became of Sin?*[15] Yet the sense of appropriate guilt is frequently denied by modern people who believe they have been "liberated" from conscience. One thirty-nine-year-old salesman (from a conservative religious background) came to his pastor, complaining of many of the symptoms of depression described in Chapter 1. He had lost interest in his work; his inertia and procrastination had sabotaged his sales, his wife and he had become increasingly remote emotionally and sexually. He slept poorly and woke up fatigued. In his dreams he was chased by monsters as he tried to run in lead-weighted shoes. After several counseling sessions, he reported having an affair with a fellow-employee over the past year, but he was certain that going to bed with her had nothing to do with his present malaise. "Everyone is doing it," he averred, "and besides we regard ourselves as having an 'open marriage.'" Several sessions later, he recognized and experienced his feeling of guilt; with his decision to end the extra marital relationship, his depression began to lift.

Much depression is caused by pathological or neurotic guilt, where the distressed person feels much more guilt than appears to be warranted by the circumstances. For example, people in their fifties and sixties who exaggerate their teenage misdemeanors, which now become the center of their think-ing and convince them of their unredeemable "sinfulness," are experiencing severe neurotic depression. When they come to the pastor, they often want to be chastised, saying in effect, "I'm no good. I don't deserve happiness. I must be made to pay for my sins."

Ellen O'Connell did not first see the connection between the onset of her present depression and the crib death of her baby two years earlier. Unable to carry on adequate sorrow work, she had not worked through her sense of guilt about that trag-edy. In subsequent psychiatric therapy, it became apparent that she was convinced she could have prevented her baby's death: "If only I had not put him to bed so early." "If I had changed his formula." "If I had not been sexually active before my marriage." If only . . . , I wouldn't have lost him. Her inter-nal conversation was full of self-blame and guilt, but none of her conclusions were warranted. Unable to get perspectives on her tragic loss and to accept the fact that crib death is still a mystery to medical authorities, Ellen punished herself con-stantly. To be sure, her earlier manic-depressive episodes did seem to reveal a particular vulnerability to loss and stress. But her failure to mourn at the right time contributed to her sense of unrelieved, irrational guilt.

To find hope again, it is important for the person in despon-dency to link his depression to any experienced sense of guilt and find a way to resolve the guilt. This may entail reevaluat-ing one's values and separating oneself from uncritically adopted parental standards as well as changing the internal dialogue and accepting God's forgiveness.

A pastor working with guilt-ridden, depressed parishioners must be acutely aware of two dangers. First, the self-blaming person tends to be very vulnerable to any authority and to anyone who is capable of activating his feeling of guiltiness. The blaming that goes on in marital conflict is easily taken to heart by the depressed person, especially when the nonde-pressed spouse suggests that he or she is "well" and the mate is "sick" and the cause of all the difficulty. Secondly, with guilty and depressed people, the danger of suicide always lurks close by. Suicidal ideas occur in about 75 percent of depressed persons, and actual suicide attempts are made by at least 15 percent.

The pattern that many religiously oriented people learn through the years may negate any theological understanding of forgiveness and renewal that the church has tried to teach. They move from guilty feeling to atonement to attempted redemption by placating and obeying, by overworking, by denying themselves pleasure, and by subtle self-sabotage or clear self-destruction. These attempts at self-redemption stand in stark contrast to what James Emerson has called "realized forgiveness."[16]

Pastoral care-givers need to have ways of differentiating normal from pathological guilt and of being able to use theological and pastoral resources to relieve the guilt and the resultant depression. In this effort they will find Edward Stein's *Guilt: Theory and Therapy*, Paul Tournier's *Guilt and Grace*, and the Linns' *Healing Life's Hurts* very useful guides.[17]

Exaggerated Hopes and Aspirations

Ironically, depression may have its source in hopes. Many of our dreams and aspirations do not really fit us and are not realizable. We may aim at a goal which seems to promise fulfillment, but the effort to achieve it may lead only to frustration and depression. Arieti and Bemporad speak of the "depression following realization of failing to reach a dominant goal" (p. 152). Early in life such a goal—which may be an ideal love relationship or a vocation—may become all-consuming, as a way of overcoming low self-esteem. The person gradually becomes haunted by the pursuit of this goal, which is usually grandiose, believing that reaching it will bring love and esteem. The individual develops what psychoanalyst Karen Horney calls an "idealized image," and is never satisfied with the finite, real self. Lynn Baker (Chapter 1), for example, believed that the accolades and acceptance she collected so easily in her early youth would continue forever. Unless the dominant goal is reached, all meaning seems to fade from life, so deep is one's investment in it. When a person comes to the painful realization that he is not going to be a great artist, doctor, politician, writer, lover, parent, or the like, he feels he has nothing left to make him worthy of love and approval and to make life worthwhile.

Frequently, perfectionism may accompany the pursuit of the idealized goal. "If I make a mistake, I can't stand myself." "I can't do anything right." Perfection brings the person under the judgment of impossible, inhuman ideals. He needs what Alfred Adler, one of Freud's early disciples, called "the courage of imperfection."

"Ego-inflation," which C. G. Jung says allows the person to think he has already arrived and needs no more growth toward the real self, also sows the seeds of depression. Lynn Baker thought she had "made it," only to have her delusion shattered. In the seventeenth-century classic *Pilgrim's Progress*, John Bunyan showed a penetrating understanding of ego-inflation. Whenever Christian became elated, thinking he had put all difficulties and struggles behind him in the journey to the Celestial City, he fell into one depression after another. His arrogance at one point led him straight into the Slough of Despond. At another point, elated after his experience at the cross, convinced that he was blessed and safe from danger, he fell into the Valley of Humiliation and, following that, into the Valley of the Shadow of Death. That is to say, the more he thought he had arrived, the deeper and deeper his despair and depression became.

One dominant goal or relationship cannot take over a person's entire life without impoverishment and pain. The individual's life becomes restricted to very narrow patterns and relationships, and his self-esteem and self-identity depend upon realization of the prideful fantasy (which probably would not satisfy in actuality): the pleasures of living each day with openness and expectancy are overlooked. Failure to reach the dream can crush a person's life and inhibit his striving. We must realize, then, that the depression is not only grieving over a lost fantasy; it is the mourning over a large part of one's life spent in the service of that distant image which falsely promises so much. "What if my whole life has been wrong?" cried Dori Schaffer in her diary. One pastoral task is to convince the depressed person that life has not been wasted and that he must mourn the lost goals and find those that fit.

A pastor must be alert as to how great a place a dominant goal occupies in the person's life. Here is where the theologian's understanding of idolatry can be of enormous value. Is it true that life without *this* goal has no meaning? Is it possible to shed the false pride and find new and more realistic values and goals? To put it pastorally, we can help the person to see that his goals and beliefs that he must be something "special" have contributed to the depression. Up to now the person has lived an inauthentic life for an inauthentic goal; he is experiencing the existential guilt which comes when he turns his back on his unique gifts. Life presents many more ways such a person can go with satisfaction and meaning. God has options; *hope is imagining another way.*

Energy Drawn away from the World by Internal Forces

What is it that happens to a person devoted to a dominant, conscious goal that isn't really suitable? Jung's answer to this question has the seeds of hope as well as danger in it. He saw the psyche as a self-regulating system, composed of conscious and unconscious realms, which attempts to correct itself when it is out of balance, as does the network of bodily organs. When striving becomes one-sided or deeply frustrated, it is likely the individual will neglect some latent deep needs of the soul. Over a period of time, the conscious life may become unfocused, apathetic, and isolated, with all capacity for feeling drying up. Metaphorically, the person finds himself in a wilderness or arid desert where nothing green grows and no life can flourish. The water of life seems to be cut off. In Jungian theory, the unconscious realm—which harbors both creative and destructive forces—gains ascendency and draws libido (life energy) from the world of conscious activity, thereby producing a "depression" (a lowering of interest and energy in everyday life).[18] Life on all fronts is blocked. Its flow is frustrated and its conscious desires are neutralized, often because of the loss of something or someone precious, or the collapse of one's goals and ambitions.

Sometimes an unknown element (or internal image) in the unconscious pulls the energy away from the world so that it can get the attention it deserves—saying, as it were, "I have unfinished business to discuss with you." This is not to say that the energy that empowered us in the outer life simply disappears, although we experience it that way. Rather, the energy is now directed inward, attempting to make a connection with the neglected elements of the self. Depression, to Jung, is not merely an unpleasant symptom; it is a diversion of energy to what is neglected by the one-sided person. *Depression is a signal which directs our attention to a way or style of life that needs correction*. Merely removing the symptom is equivalent to removing a physical pain which is signaling that some body function is out of kilter. Dreams may be an indicator of the missing direction; rightly understood, they can call the dreamer's attention to yet-to-be developed qualities.

One third-year seminarian who had done well in his studies and field work was overcome, during the final term, with great feelings of inadequacy, deep depressive moods, and suicidal thoughts. He withdrew from friends, became apathetic, and let his work slide in an uncharacteristic way. Complaining of fatigue and despondency, he went to the school's health service, where doctors put him on antidepressant drugs. He came in for counseling and, after several sessions, gradually stopped taking the drugs. His dream life increased markedly.

He reported one vivid dream of being forced into a box much too small for him by a sick woman who, surprisingly, had great strength over him. In the closed box he twisted and turned until he found a Chinese puzzle–type lock that he managed to decipher. It opened the box. It led out on to a broad road crossing a field of wild flowers and small animals. With little help he understood the dream to be picturing the boxed-in situation he felt the ministry to be for him. All his life the ministry had been held up to him by his widowed mother as a "holy" vocation, she hoped he would carry on the work of his clergyman father, who had died when he was twelve. In reality, he was living another's life story, or, as Jung would say, another's myth. The dream seemed to say that if he found the right key, he need not stay in the box; indeed, he was already, internally, in transition.

The unconscious cannot be coerced by the conscious ego, which is why St. Augustine thanked God for not making him responsible for his dreams! The counselor and the seminarian searched together for the key through pastoral conversations and vocational testing. Once the young man knew he was free to choose, released from his father's image and his mother's devouring desire for him, his depression lifted and his energy flowed outward again into productive life.

Jung reports that, most commonly, depression hits at midlife, with the attainment of maturity and most of life's goals and ambitions. A middle-aged executive, for example, very successful in business, finds himself slipping into inertia and isolation from loved ones, and into a sad mood. He has frightening dreams of death and occasional thoughts of suicide. Jung would hypothesize that changes are occurring in his psyche that demand a relinquishment or modification of his youthful goals for the sake of wholeness and "individuation" (finding the unique pattern of one's life). Instead of moving forward to a broader and deeper life, many people in midlife cling to the past with a secret fear of death in their hearts. They consequently remain fixed like nostalgic pillars of salt, rehearsing their more youthful triumphs. But as Jung says, "we cannot live the afternoon of life according to the values of life's morning."[19] Depression is the outcome of not moving forward to the next step of development. It represents a withdrawal of energy from that habitual striving until a new center is found.

Jungian analyst June Singer, in her book *Boundaries of the Soul*, speaks of depression as "essentially a religious [problem]; for it has to do with that *hubris* [pride] of consciousness which prevents man from looking beyond himself for the solution to his problems and for the meaning that lies hidden in all that he does, and sees, and is."[20] It is the function of religion to activate a hope which goes beyond ego desires and goals. The late Margaret Mead once said in a lecture that hope and hoping are the most important cross-cultural constants that characterize religion in all cultures. It is in this sense that Jung's oft-quoted words are to be understood:

> Among all my patients in the second half of life—that is to say, over thirty-five—there has not been one whose problem in the last resort was not that of finding a religious outlook on life. It is safe to say that everyone of them feels ill because he lost that which the living religions of every age have given to their followers, and none of them have been really healed who did not regain his religious outlook.[21]

The Role of Heredity

It is a common belief that depressive disorders "run in families." In the severe depressions (psychotic depression and manic-depressive illness), that theory has considerable support. Researchers, however, have found it extremely difficult to separate the influence of nature from that of nurture—of genetic factors from social learning—in assessing the causes of depression. For example, the pioneering work of Dr. F. J. Kallman found a marked excess of the symptoms of manic-depressive psychosis among the close relatives of manic-depressive patients, as compared with the general population. But later studies have thrown a doubt upon the idea that a genetic factor is a direct "cause" of such illness. A genetic flaw may mean, at most, a proneness to depression which can be offset by benign relationships and environmental support. It may contribute to a predisposition to depression and mania.

Recent studies suggest that inherited factors may well play a significant role in severe mental depression. A newly discovered mutant gene (called by its discoverers "Pc 1 Duarte"), possibly related to alcoholism and multiple sclerosis, has been identified in people suffering from the kind of psychotic depression which results in suicide. Dr. David Comings of the

City of Hope National Medical Center in Duarte, California, has observed that an analysis of brain tissue from forty-two persons who committed suicide following severe depression disclosed a twice-normal incidence of brain protein apparently produced by the mutant gene. Even if this proves to be a "depression gene," however, at this time it does not appear possible to predict when and in whom depression will occur. Having one or even a pair of the mutant genes (one from each parent) is no guarantee that a person will eventually fall into a deep depression.

Manic-depressive disorders have been found much more frequently than in the general population among the Hutterites, a small inbred religious sect living primarily in the Dakotas, Montana, and the central provinces of Canada. Significant inbreeding may play a major role in this situation, but we cannot overlook the strong guilt-producing theology which is taught in that close-knit society as another reinforcing factor.

In the case of Ellen O'Connell (Chapter 1), psychiatric inquiry did disclose that, over the generations, several members of her family had been hospitalized with manic-depressive symptoms. It should be noted that manic-depressive illness is now referred to as a "bi-polar (or biphasic) affective disorder" and is characterized, as in Ellen's case, by recurrent episodes (which may be days or years apart) of intense feelings of elation, overactivity, rapid speech, grandiose ideas, and impulsive actions (regardless of possible results), interspersed with periods of profound depression, inertia, withdrawal, and feelings of hopelessness and helplessness. The length and intervals of the two alternating phases may differ markedly from person to person. Effective pharmacological treatment, to be described in the next section, has now come upon the scene and offers a hopeful prognosis for bi-polar depressions.

Body Chemistry as a Causal Factor

Often overlooked is the fact that both Freud and Jung were persuaded that the more severe depressions (melancholia), as well as alternating states of mania, were related to metabolic or toxic factors, which made the individual susceptible to depressive fantasies and suicidal impulses. Just how these factors operated they could not determine.

A growing group of biologically oriented psychiatrists remain firm adherents of the body-mind split, viewing the body as the primary reality. They rely almost entirely upon psychotropic (mind-altering) drugs as primary treatment. Two best-selling expressions of this gospel of the physical causation and treatment of depression are Nathan Kline's *From Sad to Glad* and Ronald R. Fieve's *Moodswing*.[22] Most psychiatric practitioners, however, aware of the shortcomings and strengths of each approach, try to integrate somatic with psychological approaches to depression. For example, I highly recommend Frederic Flach's *The Secret Strength of Depression*, which views body and mind as two facets of the same reality.

Without a doubt, something of a breakthrough has occurred with the discovery of antidepressant drugs. Before they came upon the scene, only four alternatives were open to the depressed. If severely depressed or caught in a manic-depressive cycle, they might receive electric shock treatments (ECT, or electroconvulsive therapy). The mildly depressed might be given a drug stimulant to the central nervous system, for example, amphetamines, or "uppers." (These are not antidepressants.) Counseling or psychotherapy constituted a third avenue of help, but it was not notably successful except in cases of reactive depression. And, of course, the depressed could go on without any professional help at all, coping as best they could.

Amphetamines are highly addictive drugs. Their widespread use contributed substantially to the current epidemic of drug dependency in the Western world. Taking pep pills to get started in the morning or to stay awake at night for study or work became a habit for many. But often the "uppers" had to be counteracted by gulping down relaxers or sleeping pills so that one could finally get some rest—a vicious and addicting circle. An enormous number of people are caught in this cycle. More than ten years ago the Gallup poll estimated the total number of Americans taking such antianxiety and mood-changing drugs to be thirty-five to forty million, one-fourth of the adult population. Heavy dependence upon such drugs continues to be the order of the day. Approximately five billion amphetamine tablets are manufactured each year in the United States alone, and only half are taken under medical supervision.

A revolution in the treatment of psychosis took place in the 1950s when the so-called major tranquilizers (initially Thorazine, the trade name for chlorpromazine) were introduced from Switzerland. In the 1960s a breakthrough occurred when tricyclic antidepressants and the monoamine oxidase inhibitors were developed and were found to be effective in the treatment of some depressions. Beginning with a drug called Tofranil (imipramine), a variety of related drugs soon began to appear with the trade names of Elavil, Aventyl, Norpramin, Sinequan, and many others, each advertised elaborately and persuasively in the medical journals. These antidepressants should not be confused with barbituates or amphetamines, which, like alcohol, often result in a deepening of the depression when their initial effects wear off.

The use of antidepressants has been both a boon and a terrible temptation. The boon is the help that these drugs can often provide in lifting the mood of a depressed person so that problems in living can be worked through in a therapeutic relationship. The temptation is to short-cut working out the meaning of depression by attributing it totally to chemical imbalance or abnormal body metabolism. Most laity find a physical cause less threatening than those discussed earlier in this chapter, so they are usually eager to take pills for their depression instead of probing the circumstances of their lives. It is estimated that by 1970, psychotropic drugs had been used in the treatment of various disorders related to stress and depression by 500 million patients worldwide. Unfortunately, many physicians contribute to the misunderstanding of depression by their unwillingness or inability to spend time with the emotional and life factors involved in their patients' distress, instead of immediately prescribing psychotropic drugs.

The pastor who wishes to learn more about the research relating biochemical changes in the body to depression has a vast literature to draw upon.[23] Rather than review those complicated findings here, I wish to draw attention to several aspects of the research into drug therapy which impinge upon the pastor's work.

First, a pastor should know that chemical changes in the body due to drugs or illness can be a factor in the development of depression. An ordinarily stable, optimistic, happy parishioner can become depressed and express paranoid feelings with the biochemical change brought about by certain chemical substances. Endocrine treatments, various forms of cortisone, or medications used for other purposes frequently produce low moods. For example, reserpine, commonly used to lower the blood pressure of heart patients, often causes depression. In experiments, when a normal person is injected with physostigmine, depression can ensue within minutes, causing the person to feel helpless, self-despising, and even suicidal. And an injection of atropine can bring that person back to normal rapidly. Before assuming that the total cause of depression lies in a deep psychological and spiritual malaise (which, of course, can alter body chemistry), the pastor should inquire about drugs the parishioner may currently be taking and ask the depressed person to check with a knowledgeable physician about possible side effects.

Secondly, antidepressant drugs should be regarded as helpful, but not as a panacea. They may relieve depressive symptoms, but they do not cure the causes. Properly prescribed, they can help a deeply depressed person to use the "talking therapies" effectively. However, in rare cases, they have been known to lift the depression just enough to energize a despairing suicidal patient to carry out a suicide plan. And it must be remembered that 50 percent of suicides induced by an overdose of drugs occur with the use of *prescription* drugs. Research is just now revealing some of the side effects of high dosages of drugs which affect the central nervous system. Most distressing to some physicians is a fortunately uncommon condition known as tardive dyskenesia, which is manifested in involuntary movements of the mouth, tongue, trunk, and extremities.

Third, it should be understood that the new antidepressants are not emergency drugs which bring immediate relief. Their effectiveness against depression takes place slowly, over one to three weeks. If no result is seen by three weeks, the drug is not considered effective. Many depressions based on loss lift within two or three weeks without any treatment at all. It can be dangerous to take these drugs without medical supervision. Unfortunately, fewer than 60 percent of doctors give their patients any meaningful information about these medications and what to expect from them. For example, too few convey the information that a mixture of antidepressant drugs and alcohol is very dangerous, and occasionally lethal, or discuss other possible side effects.

Fourth, not enough is known yet about when a drug is helpful in the long run. Only hunches prevail. Many grief experts feel that antidepressant drugs should not be used for persons going through normal grief and mourning, nor for persons who can fairly easily identify the loss that has triggered the depression. The drug may short-cut the expression of emotions in sorrow work so needed to avoid clinical depression. Antidepressant drugs do seem to help the roughly 30 percent of people who are going through a recurring endogenous depression, who cannot relate their depression to any conscious loss or specific traumatic life event.

In the case of a manic-depressive disorder, the discovery of lithium carbonate, a lithium salt, has been a great breakthrough. It has proven to be one of the most helpful of the mind-healing drugs. A very small amount of lithium is found in the blood of normal people. Increasing the amount to specified levels is sufficient to keep the manic, or abnormally high, periods in a bi-polar depression from developing. It can keep the person calm and help avoid the panic of mania and the feeling of being out of control. It is possible (but not yet proven) that lithium therapy can also prevent recurrent episodes of depression in the manic-depressive cycle. However, there is no reason to assume that lithium has any beneficial effect on the form of deep depression that does not alternate with "high" swings in mood.

Antidepressants have helped to remove the misery of melancholia enormously, but pastors and other clinicians must not overestimate their usefulness. In our pill-gulping society, drugs have become a way of life for millions. Many exaggerated claims are made for antidepressants, which tend to give the message that we need not be responsible for our life—a pill will take care of it. Furthermore, recent research appears to indicate that certain forms of brief cognitive therapy (described earlier) are more effective than drugs in reducing the depression in chronically and intermittently depressed people. Furthermore, those who have worked out their problems in this form of psychotherapy, learning a new form of internal conversation, seem to have longer-term gains; most could manage their depressions without help after a six-month departure from therapy.[24]

The wise pastor will attempt to learn the attitudes of psychiatrists in his community concerning the use of psychopharmacology. He will look for the sensitive doctor or psychiatrist who will prescribe selectively according to the type of depression involved. Such a physician will monitor closely the dosage and the use of the drug, will be alert to side effects, and will discontinue the use of powerful chemical aids when the patient is able to tolerate the suffering required for working through the problems of living. For the pastor and physician who believe in healing, the main issue may be contained in the words of a woman who told me, "I didn't have to deal with my feelings and mixed-up view of myself and life all the years I took the medication. I never had to work through any of my problems because they were labeled 'symptoms.' Drugs were supposed to take care of them—to remove them—but the problems are still with me."

The Existential Question

I have intended, in this brief review of the many "causes" of depression to expose the pastor to the complexities in understanding depression. The shadow of melancholy is cast by many factors in our lives. Related to but broader than the various causal factors is the existential question of the meaning-fulness of life itself. Could it be that life is basically tragic? Writer Sam Keen expands the understanding of the depressive syndrome to its cosmic proportions when he says,

> The psychological condition of depression contains implicit covert judgments: nothing matters; I am a victim of forces over which I have no control; there is nothing worth caring about or sacrificing for; nothing legitimately calls, moves, animates, excites me. The depressed person lives encapsulated in a world ruled by the logic of death—only what *has been* is real; inertia is the governing power; entropy is destiny. . . . Some vision, expressed in political, economic, and philosophical terms, is necessary to save us from despair. Human intentionality must be a moment within the intentionality of the cosmos.[25]

Silvano Arieti similarly observes that the state of meaningless-ness reminiscent of that experienced by the severely depressed patient permeates contemporary culture with its loss of tradi-tional values and its inability to replace them with new ones. Arieti concludes that "a therapist cannot adhere to the concept that life is meaningless, or therapy becomes meaningless too." He asks, "If the therapist shares the feeling that any waiting is a waiting for Godot, how can he help the patient to wait for recovery, and to reacquire hope in himself and life?"[26]

As we move to explore the part that pastors can play in alle-viating the misery of melancholy, we might anticipate their work by recalling the words of that early theological therapist, Søren Kierkegaard, who held that the eradication of despair can come only when we are related to our own self and are ac-tively willing to be our true self; then the self is grounded once more in the Power which posited it. This discovery of our true self and source cannot come without courage, faith, and hope.

3. *The Meaning of Hope in the Task of Shepherding*

The recovery of hope by despairing persons is a primary goal of pastoral care. But what is pastoral care? Is it the exclusive work of the clergy? Is it equivalent to pastoral counseling? Is it confined to one-to-one relationships? My answer to these last three questions is "no." I do not conceive pastoral care to be solely private conversations with distressed individuals by the official pastor of the congregation. Rather, I see it as the "shepherding" or care-giving role of the whole congregation, led in most cases by the concerned professional clergy. It involves the mutual care of members for one another and an extension of care to those outside the fellowship who are in need. In relation to the depressed, shepherding is the judicious use of all the resources of the congregation to activate hope.

Pastoral Care as Shepherding

Shepherding is a prime metaphor for the understanding of care in the church. It has been penetratingly explored by Seward Hiltner in his explication of pastoral care.[1] Historically, it has been probed by William A. Clebsch and Charles R. Jaekle,[2] who borrow some fruitful concepts of Hiltner's. Biblically and practically, C. W. Brister has incorporated the image in the work of the modern pastor.[3] Theologically, God is conceived supremely as the Great Shepherd (Psalm 23), whose power is manifested in leading, protecting, feeding, and disciplining his people (Isaiah 40:1–11). In the New Testament, Jesus is seen as the Great Shepherd whose mandate to his people, his undershepherds, is "Feed my sheep." Purged of its rural connotations and any implication that we are dealing with a stupid flock of dependents with a herdlike mentality, shepherding is a powerful organizing image. Sheep were precious in biblical days, and a shepherd sought diligently after even one which was lost (Luke 15:4). One might even lay down his life to protect the sheep from predators (John 10:15).

The focus of shepherding is the individual person in need. But this does not limit its resources to pastoral counseling, popular as that approach is today. Nor does it ignore the social milieu in which the individual lives. A specific counseling function is often crucial, but a comprehensive care of souls can be expressed in preaching, worship, and liturgy; in small-group and educational work; in friendship networks; in a "systems" approach to administration and family visitation; and in action and advocacy groups. One-to-one conversations with concerned clergy may be simply a beginning of the process, a consultation in which the usefulness of many resources is assessed. The advantages of the total congregation are often overlooked.

Theologian Daniel Day Williams said, "The pastoral task, as it comes to every minister and every Christian, is to respond to the wonder of God's care for the soul and to share with others such knowledge as he has of God's healing power."[4] That knowledge, of course, is not merely cognitive, nor is the sharing merely verbal. Those who have been "healed" of depression are, potentially, the wounded healers who may best express pastoral care. Their experience in suffering may be more crucial than any formal skills they may possess.

At the present time, we are witnessing a great increase in the rigorous training of laity in grief counseling and in preparation for ministry to depressed people,[5] which will certainly increase their skill in shepherding. It must also be remembered that many laity are not amateurs in shepherding but skilled professionals or volunteers who are attempting to express their religious faith through the helping professions in which they work. It is the pastor's responsibility, as overseer of the congregation, to discern with them where they can best serve and to educate them in the moral and religious context of the religious community, without which they cannot represent the values embodied in the tradition of shepherding.

The image of shepherding expands pastoral care far beyond the usual definition of pastoral counseling. In his provocative book The Moral Context of Pastoral Care,[6] Don Browning, a University of Chicago professor, examines closely the current status of pastoral counseling (especially in its "private practice" versions) and concludes that, by and large, it has not been viewed by its practitioners as an organic part of the religious community and its values. With their strong emphasis on emotional and interpersonal dynamics, such counselors have expressed the healing (therapeutic) aspects of pastoral care, but have all but ignored the moral and theological dimensions which form the identity of the religious community.

When we consider that values determine goals and that goals contribute powerfully to a sense of identity, the case for examining the foundations of pastoral counseling is obvious. The values of pastoral care come out of and interact with the religious community; they are not static. But neither are they in constant flux. Perhaps Robert Jay Lifton, Yale University research psychiatrist, is right that we live in an age which requires (or at least produces) the protean person, without a stable framework for self-definition. But this understanding of basic human personality is challenged by historic religions, all of which contend that there is a "human nature" that is persistent and in which both form and vitality are kept in fruitful tension. It is a structure which makes change possible.

Healing, or the restoration of wholeness after some disabling impairment such as depression, is an important task of pastoral care. It is not the whole task, however. Shepherding in the Judeo-Christian tradition includes at least three other functions: sustaining, guiding, and reconciling, which will be illustrated in Chapter 4.[7] Pastoral care includes more than pastoral counseling; all phases of the church's life are involved. Preaching and worship, education and small-group work, confession and calling, and community action all have a part to play in bringing hope to the despairing.

Hope in the Present Tense

As we have seen, depression is frequently, if not always, born of loss, but not merely of a specific, tangible loss characteristic of grief. Rather, the common experience of despairing persons is the generalized *loss of hope*.

As a pastoral counselor, I worked for some time with a group of young adults who had attempted suicide. The word *hopeless* was on their lips frequently. As I listened carefully, I found I could often translate that word into two others: *helpless* and *lonely*. These themes surfaced repeatedly in our group discussions.

Cartoonist Charles Schultz has a character in his *Peanuts* strip ask, "Do you know what you are going to be when you grow up?" Charlie Brown's reply—which could have been echoed in this group—was "Lonesome." Fritz Perls, founder of Gestalt Therapy, used the term *catastrophic expectations* for this fear that nothing would work out. Ira Progoff, noted for his work with the "intensive journal," calls this attitude the "Never Syndrome," the conviction that one will never realize one's potential. With these hopeless expectations, and the sense that one is trapped in the present situation, the nerve of courage, risk and action is cut. Hopelessness is a spiritual attitude closed to creative imagination, new options, and an open future through which God influences life.

Generally, pastors have a positive attitude toward the word *hope*, since it is an important part of St. Paul's writings in I Corinthians 13 and in his letter to the Romans. Hope is deeply embodied in the Old Testament, which uses the word more than 125 times. But verbal familiarity does not guarantee an understanding of this slippery term.

Many modern thinkers have no use at all for the concept of hope. Albert Camus sees both suicide and hope as retreats from the courage to accept the absurdity of life. Samuel Beckett, in *Waiting for Godot*, depicts hope as resigned, ineffectual, passive waiting; the wishful expectation that the future will bring fulfillment without any effort. On Greek novelist Nikos Kazantzakis's tombstone on the island of Crete, the following words are engraved: "I hope for nothing. I fear nothing. I am free." In contrast, psychiatrist Karl Menninger sees hope as a vital process in life and in the fight against despair. Pastors must understand what hope is and is not before they can assess the place of hope in shepherding and learn to reawaken realistic hoping in downcast persons.

What Hope Is and What It Is Not

Hope is not optimism. Optimism tends to minimize the tragic sense of life or foster the belief that the remedy for life's ills is simple. According to Gabriel Marcel,[8] one of our most thoughtful analysts of hope and hoping, optimism is possible as a consistent attitude only when people take a position that isolates them from the real evils and obstacles of the world. Optimists tend to look only at the externals of life with a bland sameness of selective perception. Pessimists, on the other hand, are habitually so overcome by a negative picture of life and a closed concept of the universe, that they cannot look beyond the tragic to any possibilities which transcend the present situation.

The hoping person is fully aware of the harshness and losses of life. In order to hope, one must have had experiences of fearing, doubting, or despairing. Hope is generated out of a tragic sense of life; it is painfully realistic about life and the obstacles to fulfillment, within and without. The Christian believer cannot simply focus attention on the positive in life, since there is a *cross* at the heart of Christian faith preceding any resurrection. For the devout Jew, there is the remembrance of the painful exile, out of which deliverance comes. Unless a person passes through meaninglessness, a "valley of the shadow of death," can genuine hope be born? With this understanding, we can appreciate anew St. Paul's insistence that everyone lives by hope. *Hope is the sense of possibility;* in despair and trouble, it is the sense of a way out and a destiny that goes somewhere, even if not to the specific place one had in mind.

An optimistic attitude is largely the unrealistic product of the modern technological age. It is a faith-assumption of the industrial West that no prudent person really needs to experience the "dark night of the soul" which might lessen one's efficiency.

Jewish and Christian views of life have always assumed that in the journey of life there *are* valleys and wildernesses, exoduses and exiles, deaths and resurrections. Possessing hope, the champions of faith have not been reluctant to reveal their own desperate struggles in the "slough of despond." St. Paul, the very man who spoke so powerfully of hope, was also willing to reveal his hopelessness: "We were so utterly, unbearably crushed that we despaired of life itself" (2 Corinthians 1:8, rsv). Hope is not optimism.

Hope is not simply a desire or vague longing that the future will provide a sufficiency of what is lacking now. A great deal of what is called hope is secular culture and popular religion is really wishful thinking, utopian fantasy, desire wrapped up in illusions. It is almost totally future-oriented. The time of the present is emptied of significance and the emphasis shifts to the future, even to the details of life beyond death. Such "magic hope" is often based on projection and involves wishing for absolutes and effortless verbal formulas which promise more than they can deliver. Furthermore, such false hope fosters passivity, a prime ingredient of depression.

Many versions of the recent so-called theologies of hope have put so much weight on a future-oriented eschatology, on God's Kingdom appearing in the future, that present religious experience, empowerment, and action are discredited. One can lean so much toward the future and toward the new and novel that the present is negated. Wishful preoccupation with the future can rob the despairing person of the potentialities of the present. The genuine hoper takes seriously Jesus' warning against worrying about tomorrow.

In genuine hoping, *that for which we hope has some reality now*, even though the suffering person may overlook it. This has significant implications for pastoral care. To be sure, hoping includes imaging a future in which the possibilities of a concrete life might come to fruition. A beginning is experienced now. As one depressed woman confessed, "I have always lived as if there were tomorrow and yesterday, but no today." Genuine hoping does build on the past; it remembers the fulfillments already experienced. The Exodus from Egypt was a vivid (and constantly rehearsed) reminder to the Jews of the power and goodness of God, who had led them out of "the house of bondage" (Exodus 13:3) and established a covenant promise with them and was with them still. This past faith-event was an anchor for their hope in the present. Hopes realized in the past are conducive to greater hope.

Genuine hope enlarges the significance of the present, a present alive with possibilities (to which the despairing person is usually blind). Hope is not merely a longing for what we are presently missing, but rather a desire to experience more fully what we have already received. Where such a beginning of what is hoped for is not present, hope should be given another name. The biblical image of first fruits underlines this point in both the Old and the New Testament. In the world of the Bible, "first fruits" were taken as a representative sample of the year's agricultural produce, ritually offered to God as a token of the dedication of the whole harvest. The part signified the whole which was to come. Just so, the image is closely connected with the New Testament concept of hope: Christ is the first fruit of the coming of the Kingdom of God in its fullness. The book of James describes Christians as "a kind of first fruits" of God's creation. As in the parable, what is present in the mustard seed now will be present later in a greatly expanded way in the shrub (Matthew 13:31, 32).

While hope clearly has to be linked with one's perception of the future, *hope in the present* tense keeps us going in times of trouble. Nowhere in scripture has this been more powerfully stated than in Romans 8, where Paul pictures the pain and groaning of the world as if in the agony of childbirth. But having experienced the power and presence of the Spirit of God as a foretaste of something greater still, God's people are willing to share in the universal distress, the birth pangs, in patience and endurance, exercising their ministry of love and hope. The hope of the future becomes an expansion of what is realized, however partially, in the present. The hope of our calling is the confidence that we have experienced, as the New Testament puts it, "Christ in you, the hope of glory" (Colossians 1:27, RSV), the hope of a restored and renewed humanity.

As the Jesuit writer William Lynch, once observed, genuine hoping considers the real situation and one's unique self, strengths, and limitations.[9] Our hopeless projects are aspirations and longings that do not fit our particularities and finiteness. They signify a clinging to an idealized image of self and a commitment to an unreal future. Such illusions of hope must die so that genuine hope can be born.

Hope is not merely a wish or desire to attain specific goals that may enhance one's life. It is not enough to define hope simply as the "expectation of the attainment of goals," as Ezra Stotland does in his book *The Psychology of Hope.*[10] As I noted in discussing the causes of depression, such narcissistic "hopes" might be the source of depression if they are not realized. The maturely hopeful person remains hopeful even though specific desires are disappointed. The realistically hopeful person is able to transfer energy from disappointed hopes to better pros-

pects. Genuine hopefulness is gradually transformed into a
faith related to the sense of purpose and benevolence in the
universe.

In contrast to desire or wish, hope is not impatient. Hope is
able *to wait for the time of ripening* and not to seek impatiently
to grasp the object or goal. Waiting, according to Paul Tillich,[11]
is not a passive stance; it is an active power which does not
foreclose the future by an obsession with goals and a schedule
fixed in advance. *Kairos*, the fulfillment of time, or the ripe
moment, implies that new and valid goals become accessible to
us when we are ready for them. Nowhere is this more poi-
gnantly illustrated than in Kazantzakis's writing, when Zorba
the Greek confesses:

> I remembered one morning when I discovered a cocoon in the bark
> of a tree, just as the butterfly was making a hole in its case and pre-
> paring to come out. I waited a while, but it was too long appearing
> and I was impatient. I bent over it and breathed on it to warm it. I
> warmed as quickly as I could and the miracle began to happen be-
> fore my eyes, faster than life. The case opened, the butterfly started
> slowly crawling out and I shall never forget my horror when I saw
> how its wings were folded back and crumpled; the wretched but-
> terfly tried with its whole trembling body to unfold them. Bending
> over it, I tried to help it with my breath. In vain. It needed to be
> hatched out patiently and the unfolding of the wings should be a
> gradual process in the sun. Now, it was too late. My breath had
> forced the butterfly to appear all crumpled before its time. It strug-
> gled desperately and, a few seconds later, died in the palm of my
> hand. That little body is, I do believe, the greatest weight on my
> conscience. For I realize today that it is a mortal sin to violate the
> great laws of nature. We should not hurry, we should not be impa-
> tient, but we should confidently obey the eternal rhythm.[12]

Menninger Foundation psychologist Paul Pruyser, a profound student of the phenomenon of hoping, has said that
wishes and desires are far too specific in content and object to
be the wellsprings of genuine hoping, though they may, of
course, help an individual achieve some feeling of mastery in
life, an essential human need. Pruyser delineates the difference between hope and wish:

Following Gabriel Marcel, I feel that hoping and wishing are two entirely different processes. One who hopes is concerned with attitudes and global benefits, such as life, freedom, deliverance, salvation; one who wishes tends to focus on specific things: money, rain after a drought, expensive birthday presents, the death of his enemy. The hoper tests reality, the unbridled wisher engages in magical thought. The hoper refers to a transcendent power that has its own unfathomable purpose; the wisher bends it down to conform to himself. In theological language, the hoper is an eschatologist who lets God be God, the wisher is only an apocalyptist, who seeks reversals of his fate in which his revengeful fantasies will be fulfilled to the letter. The hoper says, "Now I see through a glass darkly . . .," while the wisher cherishes his room reservation in a heavenly motel.[13]

Reaching specific goals is often a helpful development for the depressed person, but hope must be activated on a deeper level if the person is not to be continuously vulnerable to disillusionment and discouragement. Discovering that deeper level is part of the shepherding task.

The kind of hope needed by the depressed person enables him to say "yes" to life, to believe that it is always possible to imagine another way to go. Such hope sees reality as open-ended and having resources as yet undiscovered and untapped. Certainty may be lacking, but he has the courage to act "as if" it existed.

Ira Progoff, speaking from a Jewish heritage and a Jungian point of view, describes the hope of what he calls "the utopian personality," examples of which are the biblical prophet and the Psalmist:

It was a hope addressed to the full potentiality of life become manifest in all forms of human existence. It was in this sense that the Psalmist could say, "My hope is in the Lord." The hope he placed in the Lord did not set restrictions on what God should do. The Psalmist did not specify what he hoped for. He simply affirmed his faith in the power of Life and its abundance. . . . In contrast to this, when hope is . . . concretized in a specific goal . . . , it is no longer an expression of faith in the pure process of life, which is the *Lord* of the Psalmist. . . . When hope has become desire . . . , the movement of the psyche can only follow the patterns that have been developed before. The future is made unfree.[14]

The religious person's primary concern is not what he hopes to achieve. It is, rather, what God can achieve through him, much of which might be unanticipated. The Christian wears future aspirations loosely and is not tied to past "successes," which can trap him in channels which, in terms of total development, are now obsolete.

St. Paul's words to the Philippian congregation indicate the diminished importance of specific goals in his life as he matured in faith, hope, and love:

> I have learned to be satisfied with what I have. I know what it is to be in need and what is is to have more than enough. I have learned this secret, so that anywhere, at any time, I am content, whether I am full or hungry, whether I have too much or too little. I have the strength to face all conditions by the power that Christ gives me [Philippians 4:11–13, TEV].

The most basic ground of Christian hope is the connection with that ongoing Life itself which may lead in unpredictable directions.

Hope is not simply an interior strength possessed by a fortunate few. Hope is not something we possess alone, it is basically a shared experience. We may desire, or wish, or hallucinate alone, but it requires a responsive other to discover genuine hope. Hope is born when someone really *hears* us. Hoping is the essence of the pastoral care relationship, in which real engagement, attentive hearing, and the awakening of dormant potentialities are realized. Hoping is generated, Pruyser says, *in* the relationship; it is irrelevant to ask who gives hope to whom. In *Images of Hope*, Lynch maintains that hope depends on an act of collaboration or mutuality:

> Hope not only imagines; it imagines with. . . . Two imaginations, that of the patient and that of the doctor, work together to discover and enlarge the possibilities of the situation. . . . Hope cannot be achieved alone. It must in some way or other be an act of a community, whether the community be a church or a nation or just two

people struggling to produce liberation in each other. People develop hope in each other [pp. 23–24].

In discussing the theme of depression in the Psalms, Professor Walter Brueggemann speaks of the inherent dialogue in Judaism which may change the context of despair. He says the modern dejected person

has no one to address and so will finally be depressed. Israel, always by liturgical form, has a partner to whom to speak. For that reason Israel's anger is much more healthy and buoyant. It is fundamentally hopeful because there is always a chance that the other one [the Lord] will act. Depression is never full blown in Israel because there is in the form another one who listens and takes Israel's speech seriously. In place of depression, Israel's form [of liturgy] has petition. . . . Depression is appropriate if the speech is finally monological. But Israel's form is boldly dialogical and the one who hears or is expected to hear is not addressed in hopeless despair but in passionate expectation. . . . Israel's capacity to say "Thou" is decisive. . . .[15]

This hunger for dialogue and its power in the evocation of hope is also described by the noted psychotherapist Carl Rogers:

I have often noticed in therapy and in groups that the more deeply I hear the meanings of the person the more there is that happens. One thing I have come to look upon as almost universal is that when a person has been deeply heard, there is a moistness in his eyes. . . . It's as though he were saying, "Thank God, somebody heard me. Someone knows what it's like to be me." In such moments I have had the fantasy of a prisoner in a dungeon, tapping out day after day a Morse code message, "Does anybody hear me? Is anybody there . . . ?" And finally one day he hears some faint tappings which spell out "Yes." And he is released from loneliness and has become a human being again.[16]

The psyche in its depressed and regressive phase can be destructive, both to the individual and to relationships. But a caring relationship can reverse the process. Anton Boisen, father of the clinical pastoral education movement and himself a long-term mental hospital patient, tells of the new beginnings that came with the visit of his friend, Fred Eastman. Fred had suggested, in the course of conversation, that Boisen's very suffering might become a life project in a religious understanding of mental illness. A hopeful Boisen wrote:

> Dear Fred,
>
> Your visit has meant a lot to me. *It has been for me as though I were dead and am alive again.* . . . I still feel that the story of these last twenty years is not wholly a mistake. I believe that there is in it a deeper meaning. . . . What the future may bring forth remains to be seen, but I feel hopeful. . . .[17]

With this brief exposition of the meanings of hope, perhaps we can understand how it is that Paul (in 1 Corinthians 13; 1 Thessalonians 1:3, 5:8; and Colossians 1:4–5) cannot really separate the triad of faith, hope, and love. Hope is closely allied with trust (or faith), and therefore with love. Without faith and love, hope is not firmly rooted; it gains its depth from its associates in the triad. It is "listening love" that evokes hope and grounds it in the experience of human solidarity. Hope grows in a network of human caring. In that love *(agape)* we demonstrate that freedom (from defensive, self-protective attitudes) which allows us to enter the lives of others with compassion and risking. Nothing is more hopeless than "the self-imposed loneliness of a loveless life," to use a phrase of Daniel Day Williams.

Faith is a way of responding to the present and its possibilities that draws its images of reality from past liberating events in our lives and the lives of our predecessors. For the Jew, the Exodus or the return from exile is such a key. For the Christian, it is the life, death, and resurrection of the Lord, Jesus. These images of faith are pivotal in our understanding of the freedom from bondage that would keep us from full humanity. And it is that faith, that assumptive world, that gives content to our hope. The context of pastoral care of the depressed demands all three—hope, faith, and love—linked together.

4. *The Pastor Encounters the Depressed Person*

In the course of a single week, one pastor conducted the funeral of a church leader who had committed suicide and tried to comfort the family who angrily denied that he had taken his own life; visited a community mental-health center in which a teenager from his church had been hospitalized for depression, and conversed with an anguished and despairing mother who had just been informed that her seven-year-old child had an inoperable brain tumor. Depression does, indeed, have various faces, and a working pastor sees many of them. In his work he sees people reacting to tragic circumstances not unlike those depicted in the Bible and through Judeo-Christian history. The depression and subsequent suicide of King Saul (1 Samuel) is as contemporary as today.

Pastors who are frightened by the clinical term *depressed*, thinking they are over their heads in caring for a person so diagnosed, might well remember that for centuries the care of anxious and despairing people was considered the responsibility of pastors. Erik Erikson reminds us that *clinical*

> once designated the function of a priest at the sickbed when the so-matic struggle seemed to be coming to an end, and when the soul needed guidance for a lonely meeting with its Maker. There was, in fact, a time. in medieval history when a doctor was *obliged* to call a priest if he proved unable to cure his patient within a certain number of days. The assumption in such cases was what we today might call spirituo-somatic. The word "clinical" has long since shed this clerical garb. But it is regaining its old connotation, for we learn that a neurotic person . . . is crippled at the core. . . . He may not be exposed to the final loneliness of death, but he experiences that numbing loneliness, that isolation . . . which we call neurotic anxiety. . . . The newest meaning of the "clinical" approach becomes strangely similar to its oldest meaning.[1]

Substitute *depression* for *neurotic anxiety* and the point still holds; pastoral care of the despondent has a long precedent.

Of course such pastoral care was not always effective, or even humane. We have only to peruse John T. McNeill's classic, *A History of the Cure of Souls*, to see that care often meant to admonish, rebuke, exhort, frighten, and impose ecclesiastical solutions on the suffering one. Many helping efforts of those early clergy would be considered naive by today's understanding of depression and its therapy.

As we survey the checkered history of the "cure of souls," we occasionally find a gem, a pastoral vignette which is as insightful as the latest crisis intervention approaches. *Cure*, in this context comes from the Latin *cura*, which means care in the sense of a care-fulness or solicitude concerning a person. One aspect of the cure of souls that found particular favor during the Reformation was a face-to-face confession. Although confession was no longer compulsory in early Protestant communities, it was still valued in a voluntary and personal context. Certain ministers were found to be especially helpful, endowed with a spiritual gift that enabled them to obtain a confession of a "guilty secret" from despondent souls, and so to help these persons work through their difficulty. A novel published in 1785 by one Heinrich Jung-Stilling describes such a pastoral service.

> A young unmarried woman, Sannchen, is afflicted with a peculiar kind of depression. Physicians attribute it to "weakness of the nerves" . . . and treat the patient with medications without success. The anxious family hears of a village pastor, Reverend Bosius, who is said to have a peculiar gift for "Cure of Souls" and they ask for his help. . . . As soon as he arrives he goes for a walk in the garden with Sannchen. His kindness impresses her. . . . He begins with a long, friendly talk about the love of God that is reflected in all of Nature, where every being is a thought of God. Now, what is the most beautiful of all the thoughts of God? It is love. And what is love? It is the drive of the lover to be united with the beloved. This brings Sannchen to tell him of her secret and thwarted love for Theobald and of a transgression she has committed. Having heard her confession, Reverend Bosius exclaims: "Good souls! How little you know about love!" Whereupon he starts to explain to her that under the guise of love, she has been deceived by passion . . . a "natural sex drive," the natural instinct of animals that want to reproduce, however refined it can look. . . . Following this first conversation, with her agreement, he explains the situation to her parents; then he talks Theobald into agreeing to marry her. . . .[2]

No nondirective pastoral counselor, he! Pastor Bosius used his theological belief and language and his pastor's authority in a way that few modern pastors would dare to, even if they wanted to. And that brings us to a contemporary dilemma in pastoral care.

Too often, pastors feel if they are not *healing*, restoring wholeness by a psychotherapeutic reconstruction of personality, they are not being useful. But, professor Seward Hiltner observed that at least three other functions are included in the task of shepherding: When healing is not possible or probable, *sustaining* helps the hurt person to endure and even transcend a wounding circumstance. Scriptural allusions to "strength coming out of weakness" (e.g., Paul's autobiographical statements in 2 Corinthians 12:7–10) illustrate this aspect of ministry. *Guiding* a person to make confident choices in the face of confused options, when these options seem to affect both the present and the future, has always been a key shepherding function. Values clarification is as old as the Old Testament; choosing between life and death was a major concern of the prophets. A fourth mode of care is *reconciling*. Those engaging in pastoral care seek to help alienated people (and depressed people are frequently isolated) to reestablish broken relationships with God, self, and the people of their lives. Sustaining, guiding, and reconciling often require an active role on the part of a pastor. How does he reconcile this directive stance with what he has learned about nondirective listening?

Listening and Sharing

We live in the age of the "psychological man," to use social analyst Philip Reiff's term, an era in which personal growth through psychological techniques is for many the secular equivalent of salvation. The clock cannot be turned back. The work and world views of Sigmund Freud and Carl Rogers have suffused culture and church alike with indispensable insights. For some, psychology has become a living faith, purporting to show the way to fulfillment through various therapeutic approaches: psychotherapy, consciousness raising, encountering, journal keeping, and a variety of other growth experiences in today's "meaning cafeteria." Theological language has lost its currency, and what one critic has called "psychoblab" has taken its place. New techniques and schools of therapy appear with dizzying rapidity, and with them a new shorthand: TA, TM, est, Gestalt, Redecision, and the like. Gordon Jackson, a veteran teacher of pastoral care, calls attention to the not-so-subtle shifts in the meaning of grace as pastors baptize the new pop psychologies. The "I'm O.K., you're O.K." formula for salvation (which ignores the shadow side of humanity) would be more accurately stated within the Christian story as "I'm not O.K., you're not O.K. But in the light of God's love for those missing the mark (sinners), that's O.K."

An issue that is deeper than language (which does shape our perception of reality) is whether human beings are self-sufficient, with wholeness arising totally from their own being, or whether their beatitude can be found only with reference to a transcendent meaning and a God who forgives, provides new beginnings, and empowers. Is the God-language used by Pastor Bosius meaningful today? Is the Judeo-Christian tradition still a compelling way, a viable way, of viewing the world?

Theologian Langdon Gilkey is right when he says in *Naming the Whirlwind* that in modern culture our theological language is a "ghostly language understood by few, baffling to the vast majority, and almost not *used* at all."[3] To be sure, it is still utilized within the four walls of the church in liturgy and worship, but even the participants in such rites and rituals are unable to use that language and those religious symbols meaningfully in reference to life situations. In contrast, they do use psychological language and understandings to discuss their struggles with depression and hope, as I have done in Chapter 2. Have the theological understandings of life been pushed irretrievably off the stage by the psychological?

A pastor who does not hide away in a mirror-walled, sectarian enclave, will surely have experienced the struggle between listening and sharing faith. One pastor-teacher who feels the pull of both the theological and the psychotherapeutic approach says,

> On the one hand I want to be faithful to all the good teaching I have had about listening, about empathy, and about unconditional positive regard with which I am to receive the person seeking counsel. . . . The important process of identifying with the pain and puzzlement and struggles of parishioners must not be neglected. . . . On the other hand, I want as well to share faith and Christian hope with these people, to avoid shutting off genuine interpersonal encounter and my own self-disclosure because of any false allegiance to psychotherapeutic norms—and I doubt that empathy alone constitutes such sharing.[4]

Yet that sharing cannot be glib and facile. It must be related to the pastoral situation and to the parishioner's own search for meaning. The pastor who does not use religious language automatically, as a knee-jerk response, in counseling is true to the Old Testament's reluctance to speak of the name of God at all, much less make images of the Creator.

Persons in deep distress often reach out for ways of expressing themselves that convey symbolically their "ultimate concern": They want to find words which symbolize a larger meaning for their lives. They may say, "Can any good come out of this suffering? Does God really have a purpose for my life? What does the future hold for me?" However, clergy themselves seem to be uncertain as to how to aid the depressed person's spiritual quest. While 80 percent of them see their major contribution as providing religious and spiritual understanding in coping with a life crisis (and their ready availability as helping figures), their preferred practices in providing help are not always directly related to this goal. When clergy counseling methods were probed[5] by sociologists Bendiksen and Berg in their Wisconsin study of pastoral practices, the priority was this order: (1) systematic listening and supportive visiting, (2) identifying the nature of the problem and referring, (3) diagnosing the problem and implementing therapy, and (4) calling attention to the need for a better relationship to God and providing spiritual direction and prayer.

We must also remember that there are some pastors who do not listen, and who do not identify the nature of the problem before rushing in compulsively with religious "answers" consisting of the recital of scripture verses. While these might be intended to suddenly transform the suffering person into a joyful, victorious Christian, to most thoughtful professionals within and outside the ministry, they smack of "word magic"—saying holy words to produce a change. Whether used in evangelism or in counseling, such a mechanical "sales" approach can only convince the unconvinced that Christianity is superstition and consists of programmed answers to questions people are not asking. The lack of respect for the individual manifested in such "pastoral care" is worlds apart from One who said, "Behold, I stand at the door and knock. If any one hears my voice and opens the door, I will come in to him. . . ." (Revelation 3:20, RSV).

Covenant as the Context of Ministry

The central biblical image of covenant informs the basic identity of the care-givers of the congregation, including the pastor. Professor Walter Brueggemann explains that "covenant is the dominant metaphor for Biblical faith by which human personality can be understood. . . . Human persons are grounded in Another who initiates personhood and who stays bound to persons in loyal ways for their well-being."[6]

The directed activity of the covenant-making God is expressed in an unbreakable bond of love and in seeking out those who are isolating themselves from life—the lost. Depressed persons are lost when they are locked into a negative view of the experiences of life, of the self, and of the future. In the light of a covenantal understanding, faithful human action is the effort to be an *agent of hope* to persons who are in despair, wherever they are encountered. If the persons confronted can let their lives be shaped by another Voice which reminds them of past victories and which enlivens their imagination to find new options for life, they might find hope and freedom.

An intelligent church woman I know was visiting a woman of her church who became very dejected after a long illness. Anxiety merged into depression as the diagnosis of her condition was delayed for weeks. She began to withdraw from close friends, and when they approached her, she was full of negative feelings about her life so far. "I really haven't done anything worthwhile with my life," she said sadly. After listening carefully and responsively to the woman, my friend asked her if she could remember a time when she really liked herself, when she felt useful and effective and felt life flowing strongly. At first, in her depression, she seemed not to hear the question. Then, after silent reflection, she began to light up and tell the story of her work with adult education in another community and what a difference this made to the elderly in the community. Soon she rose on her pillow, face aglow. Later she began to phone friends, letting them know she was still in the land of the living, still worried, but really hopeful about her future and what she could do, sick or well. This situation is an example of *reconciling* ministry.

Human beings, faithful to the God who suffers with his people, are also able to grieve with those experiencing loss and distress. Israel, as a people, was not reticent to complain about loss, exile, hurt, betrayal, unfairness, threat, and fear. Anger and frustration in the face of the tragic was honestly aired to the Lord. In modern times Robert Frost has caught the spirit of the Psalmist and of the early Christian writers in affirming in his poem, "A Servant to Servants," "The best way out is always through." The Old and New Testaments do not tolerate denial of the negative as do some churches built around programmed pleasantness that become, in their superficial positive thinking, cults of the frozen smile. Jeremiah railed against false prophets who would deceive a people about to be captured by their enemies with superficial reassurance. He said of them, *"They have healed the wound of my people lightly, saying 'Peace, peace,' when there is no peace"* (Jeremiah 6:14, RSV). Many would-be helpers (in the church and out) give false reassurance to depressed people. Hope comes out of despair. One must be encouraged to walk through the valley of the shadow, preferably with a companion.

Theological Guidelines for Agents of Hope

A theology of covenantal experience suggests three guidelines for the care-giver in the congregation. First, it calls for taking seriously, and together, the harsh realities of loss and suffering, and the intimations of divine grace. To be facilely optimistic in the face of searing actual or probable losses is to be unfaithful. The deep human desire to hold tenaciously to something or someone, or to some idea, is bound to bring about pain when it is lost. Overdependence on anything or anyone but God is, theologically, a form of idolatry, a common human tendency. Mourning is the painful letting-go of those attachments, and of finding a new way of relating to them, through a commitment to the Eternal.

Secondly, however, the care-giver is encouraged to believe in saving possibilities in the midst of deeply distressing events. This is the theological meaning of *providence*, which is so often misunderstood in the religious community. Providence is frequently confused with fatalism or resignation. A correcting word is offered by theologian Paul Tillich in his comment on Romans 8:38–39:

> Providence does not mean divine planning by which everything is predetermined, as is an efficient machine. Rather, providence means that there is a creative and saving possibility implied in every situation, which cannot be destroyed by any event. Providence means that the daemonic and destructive forces within our selves and our world can never have an unbreakable grasp upon us, and that the bond which connects us with the fulfilling love can never be disrupted.[7]

Tillich is clear that he does not mean that the "creative and saving possibility" must always be discerned and activated through "religious" persons. Many others can be channels of such grace and healing. We should note also that such possibilities are not given to despairing persons as a packaging solution; they are options discovered in encounter as well as in solitude. The agent of hope *imagines with* the despairing one, participating actively with the despondent in the search for new meanings of experience.

A third implication of the covenant metaphor is that, in spite of suffering with us, God will not let us go. Suffering can be purposive. From it we can learn and change and become more empathic with the miseries of others. Biblical faith suggests that what is important is not the raw facts of hurt, loss, and death, but the creative or redemptive *response* to the experience. This attitude contrasts sharply with the Stoic way, which guards against inner suffering by not being moved by it any more than necessary. In diverting attention from suffering, inner denial and emotional detachment are indispensable.

The biblical view also competes with today's expression of Epicureanism, in which suffering is minimized by gratification of every desire and living by the pleasure principle. In the Judeo—Christian view of life, it is the "suffering servant" who brings new life; it is the wounded healer who understands. Suffering, such as depression, can be a means for the *growth of the soul*. John Calvin says that if pastors are "better acquainted with their infirmity," they can better minister. In the second century A.D., Ireneaus, Bishop of Lyons, said that biblical teaching asserted that the presence of pleasure and the absence of pain cannot be the supreme and overriding purpose for which the world exists; it is, rather, a place of soul-making. The poet John Keats spoke of "the vale of soul-making" in a letter to his brother, who was experiencing depression. This phrase is a good title for the autobiographical words of St. Paul found in his letter to the young Roman church. Though he did not seek suffering, he explained its usefulness, once it was imposed on him by his opposition.

> We rejoice in our sufferings, knowing that suffering produces endurance, and endurance produces character, and character produces hope, and hope does not disappoint us because God's love has been poured into our hearts. . . . [Romans 5:3–5, RSV].

The care-giver's task as an agent of hope is to help the despairing see the possibilities for growth in their experience of depression. How can depression become a place of soul-making instead of an occasion of soul-breaking?

It is not merely private, interior growth that the helper tries to mobilize. The portrait of the suffering servant in the Old Testament (Isaiah 42, 53, 61) and the Christian way of the New Testament—which elaborates the image in the portrayal of Jesus Christ—underlines the discovery that suffering can be redemptive and a source of loving ministry. Care-giving ministry is a two-way street; the attempt to help another is always a mutual ministry. Daniel Day Williams observed "There is no minister that knows what he is about who has not been renewed again and again through discovering in others, even those in desperate need of help, a strength upon which he himself drew afresh."[8]

The covenant community (with its agents of hope) is concerned to relieve distress, but this *relief of private burdens such as depression is to help set the person free to assume larger and more universal ones.* The Christian way is something higher than freedom from depression. How can one be at peace in a world riddled with injustice, the cries of the hungry, and the threat of war? Salvation is beyond therapy and includes a growing response to God through discovery of how the whole of life, including one's inner suffering and dark side, can be brought into the service of God's love. Paul Pruyser has shown that narcissism and self-concern have run rampant through religious circles. He asks, "Is redemption an individual affair, meant for personal souls, or is its tenet the whole human community engaged in interpersonal love under God? I think this is the sixty-four dollar question about narcissism versus object-love in religion."[9]

Pastoral Initiative Is Crucial in Depression

Initiative is a unique pastoral expression of the covenant. Intervening without being asked when the occasion warrants is historically a pastoral prerogative. Pruyser has explored this resource in depth and remarks that, although health professionals may begin to resemble ministers in many of their roles, "they may become enviously aware of one ministerial prerogative which they have never had and may never get: the right of initiative and access."[10] In Chapter 1, the minister took the initiative in calling on elderly John Black. In the case of school principal Langdon Eldridge, the minister made himself available psychologically in two ways: He took the initiative in commenting on Langdon's worried look during a board meeting, thus showing attentive interest in him, and he offered time for a pastoral conversation to take place.

Kitchen counseling is a term one pastor has used to describe the majority of the brief but significant contacts he has with the people of his church and community. While structured, office-centered interviews may increase with the multiplication of clinically trained pastors, many of the parish pastor's most fruitful contacts will occur in a variety of settings—business, hospital, military installations, campus, etc.—in which the person lives and works. Brief and sometimes purely social pastoral contacts can develop into genuine encounters in which the deeper aspects of life are discussed.

The ministers of a congregation, both ordained and lay, will seek out distressed parishioners, taking the initiative in the spirit of the Parable of the Lost Sheep (Matthew 18:12–14). Such initiative is often crucial because depressed people *commonly withdraw and disengage from others* during their "down" periods. Isolation may unfortunately deepen if the mood of sadness and inertia arouses friction or anger in friends and relatives. Despondent people are often accused of sulking in order to manipulate those they love into taking a parental role with them.

Pastors who are not secure can be manipulated, too. For example, a woman used to getting her way by threats may say to the pastor over the phone, "If you don't see me within the hour, I'll not be able to stand it. Life is so empty—it's not worth living." The minister, afraid of this indirect suicide threat (and hesitant to probe it directly), changes his schedule to accommodate the desire of his parishioner. It is not easy to discern accurately a real emergency and one designed solely to control the behavior of others. If the pastor begins to feel resentful and pushed by a person's persistent demands, he may justifiably ask himself if he is being subtly manipulated. Fortunately, many communities have twenty-four-hour crisis or suicide prevention "hot lines" to which people can be directed in times of high stress when the pastor is not available.

When the dejected person isolates himself, it is self-destructive in the long run. Separated from others, he has no opportunity to check his negative interpretation of events. Feedback from those he trusts is necessary to help correct or change the world of his assumptions, the outlook on life which feeds his depressive internal conversations. Many sufferers who have escaped momentarily from the grip of their low mood testify to the importance of sharing hurts, griefs, angers, and sadness with a friend. Luther, often depressed, admonished, "Those who are troubled with melancholy . . . ought to be very careful not to be alone. . . . God created the fellowship of consolation in the church." And Samuel Johnson, a life-long sufferer from depression, irrational fears, and guilt, wrote that he could manage his fantasies in these times of misery only by sharing them with friends: "In solitude, perplexity swells into distraction, and grief settles into melancholy."

When a person absents himself from congregational participation or the friendship networks that have become a part of his fabric of living, initiative should be taken by the congregation's caregivers. Depressive withdrawal often deepens the feeling that no one cares. Moreover, people with lowered self-esteem may actually ward off the friendly approaches of visitors, and so fulfill the prophecy they have made: "You see, they really don't care." The alert pastoral care team, aware of the masked depressions described in Chapter 2, will be especially conscious of those who fade out of the fellowship to work compulsively or who are excessively hurt by some alleged slight, or who are known to be abusing alcohol or other drugs. A victim of self-imposed loneliness might not muster enough courage, or interest, or hope to contact the pastor or a member of the congregation. It is a big step to go to another for help. A person cursed with negative feelings toward himself may wonder if he is worthy of another's time and friendship. If hope is not simply an interior quality but is evoked in relationships, we can affirm with the author of Ecclesiastes (himself often in despair), "He who is joined with all the living has hope" (9:4, RSV). But often such a connection depends on the initiative of the pastor and lay callers.

Rapport Takes More than Listening

A number of very useful books have been written on the basic goals and methods of pastoral counseling, which take up aspects of the field that I do not go into here. My focus is on how the agents of hope in the congregation might best care for the depressed and despairing person, at least initially. Risks and difficulties surface in two essential areas: establishing helpful rapport and giving reassurance.

For most of the pastor's counselees, a relationship has already been established through multiple contacts in the community and the church's life and activities. If they seek the pastor on their own, distressed persons bring along a certain amount of trust in the pastor as an understanding person. When a family member has taken the initiative, or the concerned pastor has approached the distressed person, the individual may exhibit ambivalence, particularly in an approach-avoidance conflict. This is understandable, as the person may not see the pastor as a resource for his depressed state, and may feel ashamed to go to someone for assistance. I always try to remind myself that before anyone goes to a professional for help, he has almost always tried many other avenues to relieve his pain. His usual coping methods of diversion, self-control, rumination and worry, stimulation, alcohol, withdrawal, reading, or praying have not helped adequately. If his friends, relatives, and associates have not been of assistance, he may finally turn to the professional. But, by and large, he has already experienced many failures in solving his problem, which he cannot understand. His record of "failures" does not contribute to his hope for a new relationship.

The first hour or so with his helper must give the sufferer hope that this new effort is worth trying. He needs the proper balance of warmth, understanding, and safe distance within the encounter. He needs to know that the care-giver senses some meaning in his depression and knows how to proceed in helping.

After listening carefully to the initial statement of distress, I frequently ask, "How can I help you at this time?" thus tapping what the individual hopes for in this relationship. Often this is a hard question to answer since the despondent person may know only that he wants relief; he has some confidence in you as the one who knows how to help.

Like others coming to a pastor for help, the despondent person has certain perceptions of the pastor, the church, and religion. These views are determined partly by his current relationships, but they are also likely to be influenced by early experiences with pastors and parents—transference factors;

the person may "transfer" to the pastor feelings that were expressed to important figures in early life experiences. Pastors, therefore, can be virtual inkblots, becoming fathers or mothers, lovers, moralistic punishers, sentimental idealists, or competing siblings. And pastors' own unresolved problems in early relationships can shape their perception of those who come to them (countertransference). Their own needs may take precedence over the needs of the parishioner, as when the inordinate desire to "succeed" in counseling with one of the congregation's leaders makes them too ready with solutions.

In the case of Lynn Baker (Chapter 1), the pastor suspected some transference problems when she attempted to break down all professional distance, to cling to him affectionately, and to make increasing claims on him by the use of flattery, expressing a preference for him over "that psychiatrist."

What contributes most to the development of a robust rapport is attentiveness to the total person of the counselee, including verbal and nonverbal language. The minister's ability to listen well and to check his understandings of what is revealed is a crucial first step. His own warmth and genuineness of feelings is essential to the building of trust. Practically every pastor educated in theological seminaries during the last twenty years has learned the art of reflective listening, in the mode of Carl Rogers, which was the predominant model of pastoral counseling until the mid-1960s. Certainly my own experience with this form of "active listening" has convinced me of its benefit. A surprising number of people can reach real clarification of their problems and realistic decisions through this "client-centered" approach. The Freudian way of delving in the childhood origins of current feelings has not been, for me, a fruitful way of working.

However, in the last ten years I have become convinced that something beyond nondirective counseling is usually necessary for solid rapport with depressed people. Empathic listening alone is not enough in the crisis situation of threatened suicide. And even when such a threat is not apparent, it is often necessary to take a more active role by gently questioning the counselee. However, early in the relationship the pastor may withhold questions and his personal views because he is intent on listening as carefully as he can to the perceptions of the distressed person.

Why is it necessary to be more active? The depressed person is likely to talk about his low moods and sadness, given an attentive listener. Listening and responding to these brings some release, unless this is a "broken-record" revelation that has been endlessly repeated to others. However, the thought processes of a depressed, anxious, or grieving person are often so inhibited that they cannot move much beyond this focus on moods. Sooner or later, the counselor must move the sufferer's attention away from these obsessive feelings to what seems to have recently triggered the depression.

The counselor wishes to convey that he and the counselee are really a "search team," to discover through questions and exploration when the current depression started; what has been lost or what might be lost; to what extent the mood has interfered with this person's living, especially in work and love; if he is angry about losses; and his sense of his family's or friends' response to his depressed state. Reviewing such facts, traumas, and losses, which are often disclosed in questioning, brings a sense of meaning to the sufferer and reduces his fear of going crazy or losing control. It also helps the caregiver decide if he should seek additional help.

Counseling with a depressed person should move strongly, but not aggressively. Thus the pastor shows he knows how to search with the person for reasons for the seemingly hopeless situation, and demonstrates his confidence in the counselee as a fellow searcher. For example, in a grief situation, a person knows *whom* he has lost but may not know *what* he has lost in that person (values that he must somehow find again from another source). Even the beginnings of insight into the nature of the losses can bring understanding and arouse hope. Rapport with the depressed demands more than simple, sensitive listening; it requires an active approach, which will be elaborated in Chapter 5.

Conveying Realistic Reassurance

Like rapport, reassurance is required early, but it is often grossly misunderstood. Reassurance is not the common admonition to "pull yourself together" or to "snap out of it." It is not shaming by suggesting how much better off the depressed person is than other people. It is not obvious praise for vague qualities that betrays a lack of attention to the realities of life. It is not offering a cheap magical hope that "everything will come out all right," or that faith in God will pull the person through. Imagine the effect of these false assurances on a suicidal student who confided, "You say to yourself, 'This is it—it will be this way every day'—you can't face it. You want it to be over." With him, we do *not* know if everything will come out well. Cheap reassurance betrays our ignorance of the depth of the individual's misery. It also betrays something else—our inability to understand and our unwillingness to walk through the depths of the suffering with the counselee. In the Western world, we always feel we have to "do something" about a problem; we have to fix it. If people can't offer a solution, they feel like failures. Job the sufferer was rightly fed up with the false and easy reassurance of his "comforters." He said scornfully, "As for you, you whitewash with lies; worthless physicians are you all. Oh that you would keep silent, and it would be your wisdom!" (Job 13:4, 5, RSV).

What is truly reassuring? A hopeful, loving relationship and the search for the meaning of one's distress. The attentive presence of the care-giver (even in silence) is reassuring, and often is an anchor in the wind. A pastor who had rather unskillfully (and fearfully) tried to help a woman through a depression-producing crisis by saying he was sure she would come out all right was told long afterward, "What I most needed to know was not that I would come through all right, but that you and the others I respect would love me no matter what happened."

Just as the sensitive physician will not promise too much for a medication, so the pastor should make no promises about the outcome of pastoral counseling or of psychotherapy. While it is true that depression responds more often to treatment than other emotional disorders—and this can be said to the person—each situation is different. A pastoral counselor who assures every counselee that the depression will lift within two or three weeks no matter what is done is promising too much. Some will, and some won't. If expectations are disappointed, this can lead to a further loss of hope.

Religious assurance, which is true to the biblical view, does not promise specific outcomes, but speaks of the constant presence and activity of God in our suffering and is able to say confidently that "nothing shall separate us." We can demonstrate that the congregation is really a fellowship of suffering. Our intention as care-givers in the church is surely to relieve the misery of the depressed, and we will do everything within our power to provide the kind of care that will do so. In this we identify with the suffering servant of Isaiah, who could say honestly

> He has sent me to comfort all those who mourn,
> To give those who mourn in Zion
> Joy and gladness instead of grief,
> A song of praise instead of sorrow
>
> (Isaiah 61:3, TEV)

At appropriate times, especially when hopelessness seems to predominate in the person we care for, we can say some things that may comfort and *strengthen the resolve to work through and understand the suffering*. First, paradoxically, we can point to the positive contribution that depression can make to one's life. We are not accustomed to finding constructive meaning in our despondency but to regard it only as something to be overcome as quickly as possible. In fact, such distress can open doors to new life.

Depression after loss actually discloses the person's love for life and his assumption that life is meaningful and should be worthwhile. Psychiatrist Silvano Arieti says that, in his inner life and convictions, the depressed person demonstrates that he is not one of those people who consider the events of the cosmos to be due to a random collision of atoms.

Surprisingly, perhaps, most creative people have reported periods of depression just before a new surge of personal growth and achievement. Speaking of Tolstoy's suicidal melancholy, Ira Progoff concludes that "history is rich with the record of individuals who struggled through periods of black confusion until they touched something in the depth of themselves that transformed them and brought them forth into the world as charismatic figures." [11] There is often a special quality of life about those who have been to the depths and back again; they may become wounded healers.

In *The Secret Strength of Depression*, psychiatrist Frederic Flach speaks of the service of acute depression in alerting us to longstanding, self-defeating patterns that must now be explored and dealt with. We may recognize that we have been depressed a long time. An episode of depression may be a warning signal, motivating us to rethink the situations and values of life. The search for grandiose dreams and unreal goals or the attempt to live another's story is called to a halt by the mood. It is nature's way of stopping the senseless waste of energy, giving us time to recuperate and reassess life goals. Depression is often an inherent part of the process of first coming apart, then recovering new insight, and finally giving up old perspectives that no longer fit our life. The poet Theodore Roethke noted, "In a dark time, the eye begins to see."

Life has not stopped when we are overcome by depression. Jungian therapists say that the energy formerly used for the outer life and conscious work is withdrawn in depression and flows inward as if to find the center which has been ignored in all of our extroverted activity. Life's energy may not be again accessible to ego-consciousness until we have searched the inner life for clues as to the one-sided direction we have taken, or to the next step in our development. We must take what is called the night journey into the depths of the soul, which has temporarily lost its way. Depression forces us to turn for the moment from our objective tasks and to concentrate (often with the help of dreams) on what is going on within, for that is where the energy has gone. When images of new directions that fit us as an individual emerge, energies will flow outward toward the world again. Depression is the signal, then, that there is much unlived life in us that has been ignored in our present way of life. Often the time may be ripe for those things we thought we had missed in earlier life.

Theological imagination can view depression as a call of God to reconsider our life and loves. It is a forced "exile" from our former familiar and predictable life into a wilderness where a new way can be discovered. We always resist a painful initiation into a new and unknown life. Depression is the dark night of the soul; it is the soul's winter. When we experience such a barren season in our lives, nothing much may be going on in our active life and relationships, but

> The roots are silently at work in the
>   darkness of the earth
> Against the time when there shall be new
>   leaves, fresh blossoms, green fruit.
> Such is the growing edge.[12]

St. Paul can say with assurance, "God . . . comforts us in all our affliction, *so that we will be able to comfort* those who are in any affliction . . . (2 Corinthians 1:3,4 NASB, emphasis added). The depressed can trust a person "of sorrows, and acquainted with grief." Whether we face temporary dejection, enervating depression, or hopeless despair, the person shaped by the biblical view of life knows that he is in the presence of One who has been there.

Even Advice and Persuasion Can Help— Sometimes

Advice and persuasion, so long deprecated by nondirective counseling exponents, can be helpful. They can be an expression of proper pastoral authority. Given with sensitivity and at the right time, they may be just what is needed to cut through the apathy, or to enable the counselee to avoid rash decisions and further self-depreciation while in a depressed state.

One pastor encountered a woman who had had recurrent depressions through the years. In these down-spirals of spirit, she would stay in bed most of the day, failing to contact anyone or do any work. Her pastor advised her to make every effort to come out of isolation, and when she didn't on her own, he would come over at 8:30 every morning, wait until she got dressed, and take her to the church to make telephone calls to elderly people, checking to see if they were all right and if they needed anything in the way of service. At first she resisted the pastor's efforts, even though she had agreed to his request. The first morning he waited two hours for her to get up. Each morning she resisted a shorter time until finally, after she had begun to enjoy her useful service on the phone, she came willingly on her own. Several years later she claimed that the pastor's "friendly persuasion" had pulled her out of a serious depression and gave her a way to stay out of despondency. While the pastor may have limitations, he also has resources which few other professionals can mobilize. This illustration emphasizes the fact that pastoral care is broader than a counseling relationship; here it is expressed through definite *guidance.*

The healing power of service is often overlooked as therapy for depression, It ends isolation and restores self-esteem. It may well change the internal conversation from "I am not good for anything" to "I am useful to someone; I can do something effectively; God always has something I can do."

Prayer for others is also a neglected resource. Research psychiatrist Jerome D. Frank in his comparative study of psychotherapy, religion, and thought reform, *Persuasion and Healing,* illustrates how many patients are persuaded to care for others at Lourdes:

> Often the patient does things for the group, and the group intercedes for the patient. At Lourdes, pilgrims pray for each other, not for themselves. This stress on service counteracts the patient's morbid self-preoccupation, strengthens his self-esteem by demonstrating he can do something for others, and cements the tie between patient and group.[13]

A pastor can urge that the person never make a big decision while depressed, saying, in effect, "Your view of the world is currently out of kilter. To the jaundiced eye, the whole world looks yellow. In a time of discouragement, our tasks look like giants, and we feel small and helpless. We tend to look at too big a piece of the future, as if life will always be this way. It won't. The terror of the future is diluted by focusing on this day only. We can get through until nightfall. That's all we have to decide."

Another bit of advice that the despondent parishioner often needs is to be aware of his own tendency to run himself down and to envy others when he is in a low mood. The road that someone else is on always looks more attractive when we are discouraged. We are but outside observers of another's life, which has its dry and dusty stretches; we know only our own from the inside. We must watch our temptation to idealize another's way.

During a time when a parishioner has been ruminating constantly and has become, in Shakespeare's phrase, "sicklied o'er with the pale cast of thought," a pastor can remind him that God gave him a body to be used. A person experiencing healthy physical vitality can feel dejected, but it is rare for him to get depressed. He has kept a balance in his life. Alexander Lowen (see note 1, Chapter 2) compares a person to a violin. When its strings are properly tuned, they vibrate to produce sound. One can play a song of many moods on the instrument. If the strings are loose or flaccid, one hears cacophony or no sound at all. The instrument is "dead," unable to respond, as in the case of the depressed person.

A Ministry of Meaning

Pastoral care, whether given by pastors or by laity, has a theological and moral purpose that goes beyond the merely therapeutic. It is to provide a ministry of meaning. This aim contrasts sharply with what the modern person of the twentieth century may look for in seeking help: peace of mind and freedom from the annoying symptoms of depression, anxiety, and inner emptiness. When such a person turns to the therapist instead of the priest or pastor in the hope of achieving the modern equivalent of salvation—"mental health"—he is often looking for meaning. Since World War II, a new kind of patient has come to the psychiatrist's office complaining of diffuse dissatisfactions and not the classical psychiatric symptoms. While this person is usually labeled "borderline," the reported malaise is actually in an area between psychiatry and religion. Such persons complain that their lives are vague, unfocused, and purposeless. They experience unpredictable oscillations in self-esteem and frequently wonder if life is worth living. Constantly fighting boredom, they seek drama and "meaningful relationships." Too often they find a sense of well-being only by attaching themselves to strong, admired figures whose approval they crave. Without it, they often give up; they feel lost.

Unfortunately, when many therapists speak of "love" or "meaning," as increasing numbers do, they often limit themselves to the fulfillment of the patient's personal emotional requirements, and hardly ever refer to "meaning" in the sense of being a part of a liberation movement for all human beings, a movement which finds a principal source in the Judeo-Christian tradition. "Love" as self-denial often strikes the therapeutic mentality as intolerably oppressive. Insofar as it takes this view, the therapeutic community is at odds with the religious community, which sees self-denial as a necessary requirement for disciplined action in the world.

Some Advantages of the Clergy

In 1960, it surprised everyone—especially mental-health professionals—to learn that people in distress did turn to the clergy for help, and in large numbers. In that year, the noteworthy research of the University of Michigan's Survey Research Center Team revealed what American adults thought about their own mental health, what troubled them, whether they solve their problems by themselves, where they seek help, and how they evaluate the help given.[14] In 1957, when the survey was taken, one out of four persons felt the need of help on personal problems, and one out of seven had actually gone for help some time in the past. Surprising to the investigators was the discovery that 42 percent of those surveyed had turned to the clergy, 29 percent went to nonpsychiatric physicians for assistance, and only 18 percent of those needing help found their way to the office of a psychiatrist or psychologist. Another 17 percent sought out marriage counselors and other mental-health workers in private practice or agency settings. Sixty-five percent of those going to clergymen or nonpsychiatric doctors claimed they were "helped" or "helped a lot." Forty-six percent of those meeting with psychiatrists and 25 percent seeing marriage counselors made a similar evaluation. It is possible they approached these professionals with different ideas of what to expect from them.

These figures were eye-openers to mental-health professionals and clergy alike. Very soon after their publication two-decades ago, mental-health professionals, especially clinical psychologists and social workers, showed an eagerness to make contact with the clergy. Seminars held for clergy often betrayed a profound ambivalence of mental-health workers toward clergy, and vice versa. Comments vacillated between condescension and appreciation; between a recognition of the advantages of the pastor and warnings about ministers, priests, and rabbis being "over their heads" in dealing with such emotional problems as depression. Competition has always been rife in the healing professions, giving rise to frequent "territorial wars"—as in the struggle for licensing of newer helping professions and the issue of payments of medical insurance for services rendered. Now the clergy, long considered obsolete by many professionals, appeared as another threat, especially to nonpsychiatric mental-health workers. With the growth of specialized pastoral counselors, one more "profession" entered the competition in the field of emotional problems.

Our concern here, however, is chiefly with the garden-variety clergy of the parish, not with emerging specialists in pastoral care. Why did people seek the help of the parish minister so often? Three reasons troubled people in such large numbers seek out pastors have been disclosed in subsequent studies:

Ubiquity. The Yearbook of American Churches reports that of the

490,000 theologically trained clergy in the United States, 270,000 serve parish churches, with a total membership of 132 million people. Protestant, Catholic, and Jewish clergy are available in large numbers throughout the country, unlike other mental-health workers, who tend to be clustered in urban and suburban population centers. Often the clergyperson is the only counselor available in small communities.

Trust. The fact that a parishioner or member of a community can meet and come to know a minister in many different settings and roles is a great advantage in seeking help. Consequently, a person going to a minister need not blindly approach a professional, unaware of his values, world view, and attitudes. Furthermore, clergy have a network of ongoing relationships with the families of a community, through whom recommendations of a pastor might be communicated.

Identity. True to his vocation, the pastor is not solely a mental-health worker. The pastor is a theologian and, while this label might not mean much to people in difficulty, they sense that such a description suggests that *the search for meaning* is clearly within the pastor's province. Furthermore, there is no stigma in his own eyes or in those of others if a person contacts a member of the clergy, whereas there might well be if he goes to a mental-health professional. He is not a "case." He might approach a pastor for many reasons.

Several other advantages have also been noted by mental-health professionals who have worked closely with ministers. Ruth B. Caplan and Dr. Gerald Caplan, director of the Harvard Laboratory of Community Psychiatry, both pioneers in the field of bereavement and grief, enumerate other advantages of the clergy in the book *Helping the Helpers to Help.*[15] In it they describe a mental-health consultation program with clergy of all faith groups conducted over a period of several years. From their work with clergy, the Caplans would add the following advantages to those listed above:

- Clergy have a responsibility to know and care for everyone within their "flock," thus putting them in touch with incipient problems.

- Clergy often see people in crisis, the time when people are most open to help.
- Clergy are often sufficiently flexible in their use of time that they can reach someone in acute distress within hours or even within minutes if necessary, unlike other caregivers who must work within a more rigid schedule.
- The clergyperson often knows individuals over a long period of time, and can observe any radical changes that are manifested in personality and behavior.
- Clergy are not usually paid by the individuals who come for help, but instead receive salary from the community. This may be equivalent to prepaid insurance, in which the pastor is rewarded for keeping people healthy, not for treating the sick.
- The clergyperson is traditionally licensed to intervene in the lives of his parishioners when they are in difficulty. He does not have to worry about trespassing on the territory of other professionals who may be already helping the person.
- Unlike most mental health workers, clergypersons may be able to remain close to those they or others have counseled. They are able to offer intermittent care over long periods of time. Pastors are not bound by a "treatment" model which decrees that each case must have a beginning and end, after which the contract is void.
- Clergy are able to take a "systems" approach to human problems and to mobilize the help of family, church groups, neighbors, and community resources on behalf of depressed people, orchestrating a variety of helpful agents and groups.
- Even though the authority of the clergy has been eroded in the last century, they are still in a particularly strong position to influence behavior in those who feel out of control.
- Because of their theological orientation, clergypersons can provide a "sustaining" ministry in the face of incurable and long-term conditions more adequately than can other mental health workers.

- Above all, the clergy are the leaders of a community of faith and hope where stories are told and liturgies are enacted which give meaning and perspectives and identity to the lives of the well and the suffering alike [pp. 18–35].

The Caplans conclude that it is "precisely by concentrating on their own traditional functions and in developing them that ministers can make a major contribution toward sustaining the suffering in their communities" (p. 35).

5. Working with Health Professionals

In a recent book, Dr. Karl Menninger writes:

> No psychiatrists or psychotherapists, even those with many patients, have the quantitative opportunity to cure souls and mend minds which the preacher enjoys. And the preacher also has a superb opportunity to do what few psychiatrists can, to prevent the development of chronic anxiety, depression, and other mental ills.[1]

Yet the pastor's job, in some respects, is not unique. Many of its functions overlap and interface with those of other helping professions. How should the pastor relate to those professions in order to provide the most effective healing and care for depressed people? And when should he carry most of the responsibility for their well-being? These are the questions which concern us in this chapter.

Americans View Their Mental Health—Twenty Years Later

Between 1957 and 1976, mental-health services in the United States have become more effective and more sought after. Twenty years after the first survey by Dr. Gerald Gurin and his associates, similar survey was done by Richard Kulka and his associates at the University of Michigan Survey Research Center.[2] The following table shows some of the broad shifts in the two decades between the studies.

Need of Help	1957	1976
Has used professional help	14%	26%
Could have used professional help	9	11
Might need professional help	27	22
Source of Help		
Clergy	42%	39%
Nonpsychiatric physician	30	21
Psychiatrist or psychologist	18	29
Marriage counselor	4	8
Other mental-health source (e.g., social workers, crisis intervention services)	10	18
Social service agency	3	4
Lawyer	6	2
Other professional (e.g., teacher)	13	5

Three findings stand out which have a bearing on the concerns of this chapter:

1. The proportion of adults reporting actual use of any professional help for a personal problem *has almost doubled* (from 14 percent to 26 percent).
2. There is a much greater use of psychiatrists and clinical psychologists (as well as other mental health resources). Over the twenty-year period, the percentage of those

who sought such help increased from 18 percent to 29 percent.

3. While the total number of people turning to the clergy for help has increased, the pastor's *proportion* has decreased in relation to the mental health professions. Proportionately fewer college-educated and wealthy people are consulting the clergy in 1976 than in 1957. This group, generally, is turning to psychiatrists. Most patients of psychoanalysts are in the upper middle class, what has been called the YAVIS group (young, adaptable, verbal, intelligent, and successful). Only 2 percent of psychiatrists' patients are nonwhite.

How can these changes be explained?

First, while the numbers of clergy have remained fairly constant over the twenty-year span, the ranks of psychiatry, clinical psychology, psychiatric social work and nursing, and marriage counseling have swelled tremendously.[3] Schools offering graduate and professional degrees in the mental health professions are bursting at the seams. There are now at least 180 suicide prevention and crisis intervention services, often staffed by trained volunteers in the population centers of the country. Mobile mental health teams which visit remote and rural areas are sponsored by many states. All in all, the American public has many more professionals and services available than a quarter of a century ago.

Secondly, the public's awareness of and education about mental-health issues has increased greatly, largely due to popular magazines, self-help books, and TV programs. The myriad avenues of "growth experience" in our culture (often suffused with domesticated Eastern thought) awaken in many the desire for more intensive self-search. Such experiential workshops are major feeders into the offices of the helping professions.

Third, the attitudes of many clergy toward the psychological disciplines have become markedly more positive in the past quarter of a century. Clergy who have availed themselves of psychotherapeutic help—and I am one—have often found it helpful personally. The excitement of self-discovery through psychotherapy has converted some pastors to a new gospel, and they have left the ministry to become professional counselors. Others have used their new knowledge and skills to enrich their work of ministry. While many in the professional ministry enjoy their work precisely because of the variety of functions and encounters and the myriad dimensions of congregational and community life, others feel scattered and ineffective and seek role specialization, especially in counseling. Clinical Pastoral Education (CPE) now trains more than five thousand seminarians and pastors annually in clinical settings. And over twelve hundred priests, ministers, and rabbis participate as members of the American Association of Pastoral Counselors (AAPC). The latter organization has been accused of fostering a kind of private identity for the pastoral counselor sometimes only marginally related to congregations. More than one hundred pastoral counseling centers have sprung up in the last two decades. The idealization of the psychotherapist by many clergy has had a mixed effect. On the one hand, it has fostered needed collaboration and encouraged consultation and referrals.On the other hand, it has confused many parishioners who come to the clergy for a pastoral-theological perspective on their problems only to find they are faced not with a clerical collar but, figuratively if not literally, with the white coat and beard of the clinician!

When Do Pastors Refer to Mental-Health Specialists?

Referrals from clergy to mental health professionals and agencies have increased substantially in the last twenty-five years. Yet neither the process nor the reasons for referral are well understood by many pastors. Those clergy who overvalue psychology and undervalue their own role often refer too quickly and not always when it is desirable or appropriate. Those of a theologically conservative bent sometimes regard referral to a nontheologically oriented professional as a betrayal of the Gospel and so resist it too long to be helpful to the parishioner. Fortunately, we have some facts about referral to and from the clergy. Bendiksen and Berg[4] discovered that clergy most often counsel people with the following problems: personal illness or injury, marriage, death of a spouse, death of a close family member, divorce and/or marital separation, change in church participation, marital reconciliation, change in health of a family member, death of a close friend.

In general, clergy counseling is used in high-stress life events and in situations which signify the loss of something or someone the person really cares about. These stresses are, surprisingly, the same kinds of problems pastors refer *to other* helping professionals! Apparently the categories of problems listed above do not help us to discern when a pastor should refer to another.

To whom do clergy refer counselees? If Bendiksen and Berg's findings can be taken as a representative picture of clergy practices, they refer to mental health professionals in this order: marriage counselors, physicians, psychiatrists, rehabilitation and guidance counselors, social workers, and psychologists. Referrals *to* clergy come most frequently from physicians and social workers, and least often from psychiatrists and psychologists.

On what basis do clergy and other professionals decide to refer? Clergy assign great importance to "successful previous referral," and "personal acquaintance" with the professional referred to. "Preference of client" was ranked first by all of the other helping professionals, which raises a question as to how many mentioned pastoral care specifically in discussing referral resources with a client.

Apparently the most one-sided relationship exists between pastors and psychiatrists: Pastors fairly often refer to psychiatrists, but psychiatrists seldom reciprocate. Why is this? First, we must recognize that members of the helping professions, all of which have rather carefully defined standards and curricula, find it bewildering and disconcerting that they are not able to count on a common background of education and training among the clergy. Ministerial training ranges from three to six years of postgraduate work for some, to little, if any, formal education for others. Secondly, many of the helping professionals have been offended by the insensitivity of some overly zealous clergy. One physician noted that some clergy seem to proselytize and create guilt, even in hospital crisis situations. He justifiably calls them "theological scavengers."

On the other side of the coin, there seems to be a resistance to psychiatry in many ministers and their parishioners, one of whom said, when referral was suggested, "I don't want a psychiatrist messing around with my faith." While this can be taken as a defensive statement that needs to be explored, it also discloses a common concern about the world view and value orientation of particular psychotherapists. No devoutly religious person wants his faith written off as wishful thinking and projection, or as an obsessive-compulsive neurosis. Speaking to this point, Harry Emerson Fosdick once said, "What Freud called 'religion,' Jesus would have called sin!" Until members of the mental health fraternity have examined the psychologically sophisticated studies now available which differentiate "healthy" and "unhealthy" religion,[5] they cannot fulfill their professional responsibilities to their religious patients. Many psychiatrists bring to their practice an unexamined, sectarian, ideological faith and are unable to accept spiritual life as a valid dimension of the human psyche.

The Pastor's Limitations

When working with clinically depressed persons, the pastor must assess not only the condition of the counselee but the conditions of his own life as well. In his very practical and realistic book, *Referral in Pastoral Counseling,*[6] William Oglesby speaks of the limitations that are inherent in the pastor's world: (1) limitations of time, (2) limitations of skill and experience, (3) limitations of emotional security.

"This couple needs at least a couple of hours a week just now but I'm already swamped with tough situations that I'm working with. It is just lucky that I have sermons already prepared from the church I recently left, or I wouldn't be able to see them." This pastor of a large church is a typical case of the first limitation—not enough of himself to go around; a conflict in apportioning time among his various roles.

Pastors feeling the second limitation may sense that their counseling work is not really moving a despondent person out of depression and that some other kind of help is needed. Those with the most counseling training, who see themselves as effective counselors, actually make the most referrals to the helping professions. Ministers see themselves as most effective with cases of bereavement, loneliness, illness and dying, and marital and family problems. They feel least equipped to deal with severe mental pathology and with legal and financial problems. The survey cited above has shown that the other professions agree with this assessment of the clergy's strengths and weaknesses in the counseling field.

The third limitation is concerned with the minister's emotional reserve. Does he, at this time in his life, have the energy needed to walk through the valley with one who is in despair? If the pastor is experiencing a heaviness of spirit because of problems or unresolved grief over losses or defeats in his own life, he may not be able to give concentrated attention to the sufferer. Some people in depression make tremendous claims upon a helper, sucking him dry, as it were, because of their isolation and lowered self-esteem. Even a psychotherapist, with the greater ability to keep professional distance, cannot see very many of these people.

When Pastoral Care Alone Is Not Enough

Every pastor experiences situations in which his best efforts are not sufficient help. Three of the "cases" in Chapter 1 illustrate this fact. Visiting John Black in a supportive way was not enough to keep the old widower from committing suicide. If the pastor had been more aware of the signs and had probed for John's feelings about life after his losses, he might have been able to prevent the final act which cut John off from the land of the living. He might have called on a grief counseling team from a suicide prevention center to work intensively with his parishioner while he continued to give support.

Lynn Baker, the university student, puzzled her pastor by her strange behavior. When she arrived for her appointment dressed provocatively and demanded that he spend extra time with her, he sensed that the relationship was getting out of hand and needed structure and distance to be helpful to her.

Ellen O'Connell, who had suffered breakdowns before, knew she needed medical and psychiatric help and turned to the pastor as a consultant on community resources. She wanted to see him later as a counselor for her marriage and for spiritual direction to sustain her through her moods. The pastor played many roles in this relationship.

The problems of the depressive person frequently call for collaboration with a mental health professional, preferably a psychiatrist and a specialist in suicide prevention (who may or may not be the same person). When the following danger signals arise in the course of pastoral encounter, immediate professional consultation is strongly recommended for the pastor:

Feelings of unhappiness intensify, and the person continues to be depressed or hopeless after meeting with the pastor a few times. Negative ideas about the self and the future gain more and more prominence. The unhappy feeling becomes more intense. A person says, "All this talking makes no difference. Maybe there is no hope."

The person is severely withdrawn, so withdrawn that he finds it difficult to communicate his feelings or events in his life. He is slowed down perceptibly, physically and mentally.

The person is entertaining suicidal ideas. He may have attempted suicide before and is talking as if this may be a way out of his dilemma. For example, he may say, "Everyone would be better off if I wasn't around anymore," or "I'd be better off dead."

He manifests hidden suicidal intent. After being very low, the person suddenly is in a happier mood and seems calm and accepting of his situation. He is putting his affairs in order and is giving away prized possessions, as if a decision has been made. Such was the case with John Black.

The person distorts reality and expresses bizarre or irrational thoughts about events and people. She may say, "My women's fellowship is always talking about me and making fun of me. I won't go anymore."

The depression permeates his total life.[7] The mood is interfering pervasively with many aspects of his existence—work, love, thinking, decision making, physical well-being, faith, and so on.

Depression has become a way of life. The person seems to have accepted and embraced chronic depression as a style of life, is constantly justifying it, and apparently wishes to maintain it.

The person is unable to identify losses or the focal problem. Even after considerable discussion and exploration, the person is unable to pinpoint anything that has triggered the depression or anxiety he is feeling. He cannot say when he began feeling this way or what unpleasant event may be related to his despondent mood. He may say, "I don't know . . . I guess I've been down about things all my adult life."

Masked signs of depression are showing up. He has a host of physical complaints for which no physical cause can be found by a doctor. He masks depression with a forced, "Christian" cheerfulness, or seems to be in perfect control, calm and rational.

He seems to be insulated from his feelings. The person is unable to express, or has obliterated, any feelings about a significant loss in his life. He may be "numb" more than a year after his loss and cannot feel sadness, anger, guilt, doubt, confusion, or other signs of normal grief.

The pastor feels manipulated. Though this might be the pastor's own problem in part, he may also have "objective" evidence (as in the case of Lynn Baker) that the person may be using the low mood and suicidal threats to indirectly control the people in his environment. He is able to change his mood when his wishes are acceded to.

All of these danger signals could be signs of severe depression or of deeply ingrained neurotic patterns that will not ordinarily be helped by pastoral counseling or care alone.

Two decades ago the pastor would have been advised to quickly "refer" the person with these characteristics (meaning referral for treatment). The more useful approach now is for the pastor to seek *professional consultation* first, except in clearly suicidal emergencies when action must be taken to get the person immediate medical help. A consultation may result in a variety of plans; for example, short-term referral for diagnostic assessment, long-term referral for hospitalization or medical and psychiatric treatment, the creation of a "treatment team" in which the pastor plays a part, or pastoral counseling accompanied by intermittent consultations and/or supplementary medical care.

When the Despairing Person Threatens Suicide

One of the most crucial tasks in caring for depressed people is assessing suicide risk. Self-destructive thoughts cross the minds of at least three-quarters of despondent people, but the great majority do not complete the act. However, of all the persons who end their lives by self-inflicted, self-intentioned death, perhaps 60 percent are judged to be "clinically depressed," as described in Chapter 2.[8] The risk is always present, and should be in the forefront of any pastor's mind when encountering depressed parishioners.

It should not be assumed that health professionals or fellow clergy have a special immunity from suicide because of their training. Indeed, physicians have the highest suicide rate of any profession, more than three times the national average. And psychiatrists have the highest incidence of suicide within the medical fraternity. The number of publicly acknowledged physician suicides each year is equivalent to an entire graduating class from a good-sized medical school. Many clergy, too, commit suicide. The rate is rising, but it is still considered low among the professions. We cannot forget that healers frequently need healing too.

Views about suicide have varied throughout Jewish and Christian history. Neither the Old nor the New Testament explicitly forbids suicide. The Jewish defenders of Masada and the early Christian martyrs justified suicide in the face of military defeat, potential slavery, or personal attack and rape. Over the centuries, however, suicide came to be regarded as a seriously sinful act. In contemporary congregations are those who adhere to that belief as well as those who claim that every person has a right to end his own life. But there is still a strong moral stigma applied to suicide, if we can judge by the number of relatives who will refuse to talk with the pastor about a suicide in their families.

Whatever one's theological or philosophical views on the matter, there is a solid, practical basis for the decision to try to prevent suicide when we can. *Most individuals who are acutely suicidal are so for a relatively short time, and even during this time they are extremely ambivalent about living and dying.* They desire to live and, at the same time, they desire to die. If these persons are helped to delay the act of suicide, after a time they can often reperceive their situation and voluntarily and eagerly live useful lives. Those who are no longer ambivalent will not seek out the pastor, call suicide prevention hot lines, or come to emergency rooms of hospitals after overdosing on drugs.

The general message of the person threatening or attempting suicide is a cry for help—"please save me from my hopelessness . . . help me to find something to live for." The specific words the pastor might hear in counseling are variations of the following:

- I just can't stand the pain anymore.
- Without Jim, I can't go on.
- My folks will be sorry when I'm dead.
- John is gone . . . it'll be two years tomorrow . . . and I want to join him.
- Without the use of my hands, why should I go on?
- You won't be seeing me around any more.
- I wonder how they'll manage without me.

Contrary to a popular misconception that people who talk about suicide don't commit it, fully 80 percent of those committing suicide have given warnings of their intent to someone they know. If the person had been completely decided on suicide, he probably would not have given such hints.

Often the balance of life- and death-wishes is so precarious that it takes very little to weight the scales one way or the other. An unusually perceptive veterinarian received a call from a woman who wanted to make arrangements to board her dog "indefinitely." He inquired into the reason for this odd request and soon recognized that he was talking to a depressed person who intended to take her life. After encouraging the woman to talk about her depression, he convinced her that her dog needed her personal care and would pine after her. Thus, he tipped the scales toward life and was able to arrange for her to see a counselor in a crisis intervention center.[9]

When the pastor gets the slightest hint of suicidal ideas, he should *clearly ask* about any suicidal intentions the person might have. This is no time for glib reassurance; it is the time for the clarification of ideas and plans. Don't be afraid to come right out and ask, "Do you feel bad enough to kill yourself?" or "Are you planning to kill yourself?" or "Are you so upset that you are thinking of suicide?" Potential helpers of suicidal persons often fail to use this important tool of direct questioning in the false belief that they might plant the idea of suicide. On the contrary, experience in suicide prevention centers reveals that suicidal people are relieved when someone is sensitive enough to verbalize the despair they are feeling. They have already been thinking about suicide. And they may say "yes" with a great sense of relief.

Further direct questions are needed. "Why do you want to kill yourself?" "Have you tried in the past?" "What do you think the reaction of people you know would be?" "Do you have a plan for ending your life?" "What are you thinking of doing?" The person who has a well-thought-out plan—naming time, place, and method—with an available method, is an immediate, high-risk candidate for suicide.

Ask as much as possible about the person's intent. Some people really intend to die, and others hope to bring about a change in their circumstances through a suicide attempt. Jungian analyst James Hillman says that suicide is always "the urge for hasty transformation."

In a high-risk situation, no pastor should try to be "objective" or try to give theological arguments to persuade the person from taking his life. The pastor must let the person know that he cares for him and doesn't want to lose him—that it really matters to the pastor that he lives and has a chance to find options to his problem. The pastor must state unequivocally that if he kills himself it would be impossible to work with him at other ways of getting through his hopelessness.

After the pastor has listened carefully and responded in a way to show the person he really does care and is trying to understand, a trust begins to develop in the relationship. He goes with the sufferer into the meaninglessness and hopelessness of his life, giving assurance that he would like to look at the depressed person's problem with him and explore other ways of solving it, if they can talk further together. This confidence tends to plant a seed of hope. Hope is imagining another way.

The pastor further asks the would-be suicide to promise not to take any steps toward taking his own life until they have talked together again; the pastor really wants him to stay alive so they can work together to find ways to overcome his despair. Surprisingly, such a promise is one of the strongest deterrents to self-destruction.

Sometimes even more direct action is necessary. Where possible in a suicidal crisis, the pastor will try to alert family, friends, neighbors, or rescue squads to the danger. He may drive the person to a crisis center or hospital.

When a suicide does occur, it inevitably causes a crisis in the lives of many survivors: children, spouse, parents, other relatives, friends, and anyone closely associated with the dead person. The pastor has a crucial ministry to those survivors, which can be enhanced by taking courses in grief counseling at a seminary, a university, or a local suicide prevention center. In addition to conducting a sensitive funeral, he must handle any mixed reactions in the survivors. He must help them to acknowledge the suicide rather than to deny or rationalize it. He must assist them in expressing a variety of feelings: sadness, that this life has ended so tragically; anger, that the suicide has left them abandoned; guilt, since they "should have" prevented the suicide, or because they feel relieved that the person is now out of their life; blame, since there is frequently a search for a scapegoat upon whom to project responsibility. Post suicide counseling is crucial because ideas of suicide and suicide attempts occur more frequently among survivors of a suicide than among survivors of a nonsuicidal death.

The risk of suicide brings us to recognize the importance of professional consultation to aid the work of pastoral care.

The Meaning and Value of Consultation

As a front-line worker with depressed people, the pastor is bound to feel the need for collaboration with mental health professionals in many difficult situations. The advice to "refer immediately if you feel you are over your head" is not wise counsel for two reasons. First, if a person comes to the pastor on his own, the pastor has been chosen as the major resource for working through his problem. To refer too quickly, and without adequate reason, may make the person feel rejected.

Secondly, an intermediate step between pastoral counseling and referral is now available to many pastors: professional consultation. The usual pattern is for a pastor, or group of pastors, to contract professionally with a mental health specialist for advice in working with parishioner-counselees. The purpose is not psychotherapy for the minister. As described in the major work on consultation to pastors, *Helping the Helpers to Help*, by Ruth B. Caplan,[9] the goals of such discussion are three: first, to help the minister be better able to satisfy the parishioner's needs; second, to enable the minister, as a result of his experience with this case, to gain sufficient knowledge, skill, and objectivity to handle similar future situations on his own; and third, to help the pastor differentiate those cases which a competent minister might handle and those best treated by a mental health specialist. As Caplan writes,

> Consultants do not persuade clergymen to "treat" mental disturbances, although ministers may already cope routinely and successfully with many forms of emotional illness, such as depression and obsessional neuroses among their parishioners. Rather, they try to help ministers differentiate between those conditions that are best

treated by a mental health specialist, and other cases, which may *appear* alarming but which may be effectively dealt with by a competent clergyman. Without sufficient experience and support, a minister might refer many of these latter conditions to psychiatric services, unnecessarily subjecting parishioners to waiting lists and other obstacles, and helping to further clog access to mental health facilities for more serious cases. He may also help his parishioner to assume unnecessarily the expense, both financial and emotional, of becoming a "patient." On the other hand, some clergymen mistake psychoses for milder conditions. They may try to manage them alone, and may thereby inadvertently deprive a person of the medical treatment that might cure him [p. 40].

After work with a consultant, a minister should come to know with more confidence when to refer directly to local medical services or crisis intervention agencies and when to collaborate first on the way he is handling the situation. Rarely does such a consultant become a referral source; however, the community's resources and processes of referral can be discussed with the consultant. The following questions about referral should be raised in a consultative session:

- How shall the pastor relate his referral decision to his counselee? Shall he be candid about his reasons for considering referral?
- What if the counselee is unable or unwilling to carry out the pastor's recommendation?
- How should the counselee be involved in an appraisal of his own problem and in the selection of a person or place to whom he is referred?
- What information should the pastor transmit to the professional person who will receive the counselee? Should the counselee be apprised of such a report and its contents?
- How can the pastor work with friends, relatives, and family of the person who are resistant to the idea of the referral?
- How can the pastor check the effectiveness of a specific referral?
- How can the pastor continue his care of the person referred in such a way as to enhance rather than interfere

with the treatment process? How does he maintain his distinctly pastoral role?

The mental health consultative process is being used by an increasing number of ministers, and this special service is often budgeted by churches and judicatories for the pastor's use. If the area in which a pastor is located is rich in resources, consultations can take place in periodic individual or group sessions with resident psychiatrists, crisis intervention experts, or trained hospital chaplains. For example, in San Francisco's Presbyterian Hospital, Chaplain George Fitzgerald not only has a consultation service for pastors working with difficult family problems, but works conjointly with whole families of chronically ill or disabled patients to enhance their abilities to cope with a potentially depressive situation. In areas remote from such resources, state-sponsored mobile health teams can be consulted and telephone consultations with or written communications to state or regional departments of mental health are often possible. The minister who is the only professional in a small community (where he is often viewed as *the* mental health expert in residence) will find substantial help in recognizing mild and severe psychopathology in a useful book by Robert Mason and his associates: *The Clergyman and the Psychiatrist—When to Refer*.[10]

In the future shape of pastoral ministry, mental health consultation will play a crucial role. Working with the depressed, a pastor may find it is indispensable. The key role of the consultant has yet to be acknowledged by most clergy. Properly trained mental health consultants to ministers "try to ensure that while ministers incorporate greater psychological sophistication into their traditional religious role, they do not subordinate the values and techniques of their ministry to the newly discovered insights from another field."[11]

Where Pastors Can Help

We have examined the signs of severe depression which require consultation and/or referral. Pastoral counseling will be effective with people who are experiencing a mild or moderate depression and are generally able to pinpoint the events or losses in their lives to which it is related. According to psychiatrists Arieti and Bemporad, in these situations,

> (1) the depression is not so intense as to affect the total personality of the patient. (2) The patient wants to get rid of the depression. (3) Suicidal ideas are not a predominant feature. (4) The patient responds, although to a moderate degree, to cheerful aspects of the environment and to attempts to comfort him. (5) The psychosomatic symptoms are different inasmuch as . . . the loss of appetite is not excessive [and] . . . the insomnia is relatively mild.[12]

The situation of Langdon Eldridge, described in Chapter 1, would have met these criteria. Indeed, Langdon responded well in five hours with the pastor, gaining perspective on his situation and making some important decisions about his future.

"George Hoffman" is another depressed person who was helped through pastoral counseling alone. The pastor had spoken on life transitions at a Rotary meeting and was approached by George, a successful businessman in his late forties, who wanted a conference with him. In the initial session, George reported with tears in his eyes that his only son had dropped out of medical school to join a commune and learn carpentry. He was both angry at his son's decision and guilty that he had not been the kind of companion and father who could have conveyed the "proper values" to his boy. His depression was making his life miserable, he said, and he described his sleeplessness, his inability to make decisions at his brokerage firm, his growing distance from his wife, and an apathy and sadness that even his associates at work remarked about.

In subsequent contacts, the pastor enabled George to discover that his son's decision had triggered his own midlife crisis: His current success was bringing him no satisfaction after years of hard work. In the face of his son's freedom to change his direction, George had to evaluate his own "stuckness" in the course of his life and career. Recently his own father, the founder of the brokerage firm, had died, and George was confronted with his own mortality and his awareness of how much his life had been a reflection of his father's dreams. This was a case of "transitional depression," and pastoral counseling was appropriate for working it through (see the reading list).

Working with the Spouse or Family of the Depressed

Whether the pastor is secondary or primary in counseling the depressed person, he can always have a key role in the care of the family. The spouse, family, or primary group is usually involved in some way with the individual's depression. The extreme view of some systems-oriented family therapists is that the depression is *always* caused by the current family relationships. After working in family therapy for many years and doing research on specific problems and their relation to family dynamics, I cannot take this doctrinaire point of view.[13] In marital separation, for example, it is very difficult to determine whether the separation produced the depression or whether symptoms of depression developed earlier in life produced the conflict and separation. Robert Weiss, a leading expert on marital separation, says:

> Depression can burden a marriage in many ways: the depressed spouse is likely to appear ungratified by the marriage, to have limited energy for the give and take of family life, and to be sufficiently withdrawn to make the other spouse feel uncared for. The failing marriage may then produce an upsurge in quarreling that itself fosters depression, even without separation having taken place.[14]

Marital separation can increase the likelihood of depression. It is easy to blame the rejection on oneself and to become convinced of one's own unacceptability. One woman said to her pastor, "If Ed, who knows me better than anyone else, wants to leave me, anyone who knew me well would think the same way." And the downward spiral of negative internal conversation is accelerated. Additional depressive consequences of marital separation include the loss of social standing in the church; lessened access to friends; and the possible loss of income, property, savings, home, and access to one's children. Suicidal fantasies are common when people are so deprived. The pastor's marriage and family counseling (usually two-thirds of his counseling load) will involve a great deal of the dynamics of depression discussed in this book.

Pastors in contact with the families of depressed persons must deal with the misunderstandings many families have about depression (and suicide attempts) and the relevant forms of therapeutic help. "I'm ashamed that my husband broke down. He's intelligent and he knows the Lord. How could he become depressed?" This attitude is all too common among Christians. And it may be up to the pastor, on the basis of his knowledge of depression, to explain what is going on, the relationship of those dynamics to his religious life (see Chapter 7), and the necessity of psychiatric help. The reassurance which was suggested in Chapter 4 may be especially important for families as well as for counselees when the pastor seeks to explain the potential growth that can occur in depression.

When he knows the family well, the pastor may sense that disturbed relationships in the family unit may have contributed to the depression of one of its members. A family that prohibits any direct expression of anger by its members to each other may make them vulnerable to depression. Giving contradictory or "double-bind" messages also contribute to discouragement and depression. For example, a child may be expected to succeed socially outside the family, but at the same time be expected to fail so that he will not become independent of the family unit. Such a child may later fear abandonment when he does succeed, and become depressed. When he sees these kinds of family patterns, a pastor might well consider referring the family to a family therapist.

The care of the family when one of its members is depressed or hospitalized is a gift which is often overlooked. Many people may ask a wife, "How is Bob doing?" but only the most sensitive souls ask, "How are *you* doing?" The burden is often great for those not afflicted who are trying to care for the one who is.

What is it, in summary, that the care-givers of the congregation can do for the family of the depressed person?

- They can show through their attention that someone cares that the family's life has been changed by the suffering one member is undergoing.
- They may be able to reassure the family by explaining the dynamics of serious depression and the variety of treatments for it so that they might aid in the recovery process. Leonard Cammer's book *Up from Depression*[15] gives very helpful suggestions to relatives on how to deal with depressive reactions at home.
- They are often essential in describing to the family the precautions that must be taken with a suicidal person: the need for someone to be with him at all times or find other ways of protecting him as long as he holds on to the desire to die.
- They may be helpful in convincing resistant relatives that the person should be hospitalized. When possible, this decision needs to be made collaboratively, with agreement among the patient, the family, and the doctor. The pastor might be a facilitator of that joint decision.
- They can help a spouse understand the unpredictable behavior, confusion, vacillating emotions, and frequent bouts of depression that sweep over a mate in the midst of an attempt to restructure a new life. The "worse" aspect of the "for better or for worse" vow of marriage can be experienced during such a transition.

Contemporary pastoral care of the depressed person inevitably involves collaboration with health professions. Even when the primary care of depressed persons is in the hands of health professionals, the pastor may play an indispensable role in his ministry to families. Working as a team, pastors and the medical community can find great rewards in seeing the fading of seemingly endless sorrow and the dissolution of patterns of life which have stifled joyful and hopeful living.

6. *Pastoral Counseling Strategies for Activating Hope*

Any pastor needs to decide whether to counsel with a depressed person and his family, or whether to confine himself to general pastoral care and start-up contacts, as described in Chapter 4. *Counseling* should be carefully defined in the pastor's mind as a specific kind of pastoral relationship in which there is a "contract" (not necessarily written or accompanied by economic considerations) to set aside specific times and a place to work on the counselee's problem. It is an agreement to become a member of a "search team" for a specific number of sessions (preferably four to six) with the specific objective of helping the depressed person find hope and momentum again.

Any member of the clergy is likely to encounter three kinds of depressed people. First are the chronically depressed, sometimes psychotic, who have appropriated depression as a way of life. Typically, they have been to many people for help—doctors, psychologists, family service workers, friends, and other pastors—but little if any progress has been made. They "burn out" the person who chooses to work with them over a long period of time. Second are the severely and acutely depressed, who need medical or psychiatric treatment as the primary form of help, with pastoral care being supplemental. Third are the mildly or moderately depressed, whose low moods are related to identifiable kinds of stress or losses. In two to six counseling sessions, a pastor can often help them begin to move their lives creatively into the future. An initial session with any of the three groups of people should be regarded as a consultation, not as counseling.

The following strategies are designed to be used, as appropriate, with the third group. They have been utilized effectively in individual, group, and retreat contexts. Any pastor can learn to adapt them to his style and to invent variations on these counseling approaches.

Helping the Depressed Person to Identify and Acknowledge Losses

The ability to pinpoint the event or events that triggered depression signifies the kind of depression that generally responds well to counseling. Once the crucial loss has been identified and acknowledged, the sufferer often experiences a feeling of relief and of increased control over his life. Sometimes simple questions are enough to help the person spot those life changes or anticipated losses and to explore them. "How long have you felt this way? When did it start?" "Can you tell me what happened at that time to change your mood?" "Had you ever experienced a deep sadness like this before?" "Did you try to find help at that time? What did you do?" "How did it come out?" And in the case of anticipated loss, "Now that you've had this heart attack, how do you think life will change for you?" If the counselee is very fearful, "What is the worst thing you can imagine happening?"

When the pastor asked Ellen O'Connell what happened to make her feel so upset and depressed, she was able to point to the baptism of the baby in church as the triggering event. But at first she did not connect this symbolically with the crib death of her own baby two years earlier. She needed to make that connection in order to work out the grief that was discontinued too early.

In order to be a triggering event, a loss must have deep significance for the person, affecting his identity or way of life. Not all losses can be related to a particular event, however. The dawning realization of a gradual disaffection of one's mate, the perfectionist's constant dissatisfaction with his performance, or the gap between what one hopes for and what one receives from interpersonal relationships may bring on episodes of depression. We can document the loss of "the dream" in the male midlife crisis, in which a flawed success or outright failure negates the individual's huge past effort to achieve a goal. The slow erosion of the excitement or meaning in life may not work like a triggering event for depression, but it certainly contributes to its development. The slow hurts of disappointment and disillusionment as well as the total impact of specific, stressful events are losses important to identify and acknowledge.

When a person has difficulty exploring the losses and hurts of his life, I have found the Holmes-Rahe Social Readjustment Rating Scale,[1] given to individuals and groups, a very helpful starting point. As a yardstick for personal stress, it can launch a depressed person on a helpful examination of the recent and "forgotten" life events that may have precipitated the depression. In effect, this scale ranks forty-three critical changes in life according to the degree of adaptability and adjustment they usually require. After interviewing more than five thousand persons about life events which had caused them stress, Dr. Holmes and his associates at the University of Washington rated these changes on a scale of 0 to 100 Life Change Units

(LCUs). The number of LCUs represent the severity of impact on the average person. Of course, each individual will differ in his reactions to these events and whether they threaten his self-esteem or ability to cope. It surprises many people that "joyful" events, as the society defines them, can be the source of more stress than some obvious losses. The Holmes-Rahe scale is shown below.

Life Event	Life Change Units
1. Death of spouse	100
2. Divorce	73
3. Marital separation from mate	65
4. Detention in jail or other institution	63
5. Death of a close family member	63
6. Major personal injury or illness	53
7. Marriage	50
8. Being fired at work	47
9. Marital reconciliation with mate	45
10. Retirement from work	45
11. Major change in the health or behavior of a family member	44
12. Pregnancy	40
13. Sexual difficulties	39
14. Gaining a new family member (e.g., through birth, adoption, oldster moving in, etc.)	39
15. Major business readjustment (e.g., merger, reorganization, bankruptcy, etc.)	39
16. Major change in financial state (e.g., a lot worse off or a lot better off than usual)	38
17. Death of a close friend	37
18. Changing to a different line of work	36
19. Major change in the number of arguments with spouse (e.g., either a lot more or a lot less than usual regarding child-rearing, personal habits, etc.)	35
20. Taking on a mortgage greater than $10,000 (e.g., purchasing a home, business, etc.)	31
21. Foreclosure on a mortgage or loan	30
22. Major change in responsibilities at work (e.g., promotion, demotion, lateral transfer)	29

23. Son or daughter leaving home (e.g., marriage, attending college, etc.) — 29
24. In-law troubles — 29
25. Outstanding personal achievement — 28
26. Wife beginning or ceasing work outside the home — 26
27. Beginning or ceasing formal schooling — 26
28. Major change in living conditions (e.g., building a new home, remodeling, deterioration of home or neighborhood) — 25
29. Revision of personal habits (dress, manners, associations, etc.) — 24
30. Troubles with the boss — 23
31. Major change in working hours or conditions — 20
32. Change in residence — 20
33. Changing to a new school — 20
34. Major change in usual type and/or amount of recreation — 19
35. Major change in church activities (e.g., a lot more or a lot less than usual) — 19
36. Major change in social activities (e.g., clubs, dancing, movies, visiting, etc.) — 18
37. Taking on a mortgage or loan less than $10,000 (e.g., purchasing a car, TV, freezer, etc.) — 17
38. Major change in sleeping habits (a lot more or a lot less sleep, or change in part of day when asleep) — 16
39. Major change in number of family get-togethers (e.g., a lot more or a lot less than usual) — 15
40. Major change in eating habits (a lot more or a lot less food intake, or very different meal hours or surroundings) — 15
41. Vacation — 13
42. Christmas — 12
43. Minor violations of the law (e.g., traffic tickets, jaywalking, disturbing the peace, etc.) — 11

The figures in items 20 and 37 would probably have to be updated to represent current economic realities.

The cumulative impact of the changes on this scale can be judged by adding the LCU scores for events occurring in a single year. After an exploration of the medical histories of these five thousand people, a link was found between the amount of stress experienced and the probability of health changes, both physical and emotional. When the changes over a single year totaled 150 to 199 LCUs, the individuals were judged to be experiencing a "mild" life crisis—and the medical reports showed that 37 percent of them experienced health problems. A "moderate" crisis was indicated by a score between 200 and 299, and the correlation with a change in health rose to 51 percent. When the LCU scores topped 300 points—the dimensions of a "major" crisis—almost 80 percent fell ill and/or had psychological problems the following year.

I have found church groups and individuals able to explore their life changes through this scale. When they locate the events related to their depression, they are often perceptibly relieved. Now their mood has a meaning.

Exploring the Meaning of the Loss

More important than the loss itself may be its meaning to the person and his reaction to it. Sometimes a person is not clear on exactly what he has lost and how this has affected his life. At first, Langdon Eldridge (Chapter 1) was only acutely aware of his unhappiness in his new job. Then it began to dawn on him what he was missing. Unless he discovers the meaning of the loss, no efforts can be made to restore those meanings and fulfill those frustrated needs in the future.

C. Murray Parkes, a noted English researcher on bereavement, illustrates the many unforeseen changes and losses that are experienced when a mate dies:

> The loss of a husband . . . may or may not mean the loss of a sexual partner, companion, accountant, gardener, baby-minder, audience, bed-warmer, and so on, depending on the particular roles normally

performed by this husband. Moreover, the loss brings other secondary losses in its train. The loss of a husband is usually accompanied by a considerable drop in income, and this often means that the widow must sell her house, give up her job (if she has one), and move to a strange environment. The need to learn new roles without the support of the person upon whom she has come to rely, at a time when others in the family, especially children, are themselves bereaved and needing support, can place a major burden on a woman over and above the fact of the bereavement itself.[2]

Pastors are in a crucial position to follow up on the long-range impact of losses with the help of the lay ministers of the congregation, impacts which may not be realized until months after a funeral. It may not be until well after the death of a loved one that the bereaved comes to discover and appreciate the contributions, the "gifts," that person made to life. During the mourning period (and perhaps much later for the depressed person), the pastor or lay grief counselors of a church may help the bereaved to review the details of the life that was shared with the deceased. The one who needs to grieve should also be encouraged to speak about the actual circumstances of the death in great detail; this is something the mourner may need to do over and over again to learn to say goodbye.

Many life changes mean essentially a loss of control over one's life, and this becomes a serious contribution to depression if such control is a strong value. Where one's need for autonomy is exaggerated and has not been balanced with some way to express dependency, such a loss is the deepest threat imaginable. A recent study of cancer patients showed that many manifested a marked depression due to feelings of hopelessness, the lack of a future, and the feeling that control had passed from their hands. In old age, a sudden change from being in charge of one's life to the necessity of giving control to another—as in a nursing home—results in a very high suicide rate. Especially when the older person has been a self-sufficient high achiever and has carried considerable responsibility, the loss of internal control can be traumatic and depressing. Fifty to sixty percent of formerly *active* elderly people who have been institutionalized die within a year, many simply giving up. Having lost control, they cease fighting and lose hope. (This is one reason we should maintain older people in their own homes as long as possible.) A shy "Aunt Bessie," who had never made important decisions by herself is not as subject to demoralization and depression when she must become dependent. Professor James Thorson of the University of Nebraska Gerontology Program concludes that in old age it is often better to be a never-was than a has-been.

Working Through Delayed Grief Reactions

The person who has delayed grief or sorrow work often becomes depressed, as we have seen. He is often apathetic and numb instead of sad when the pastor meets him. He has not been helped to work through his grievous hurt when it occurred. The person in the "positive-thinking" church or a rational-technical society feels compelled to be in control and to bear up bravely. He tries to put his loss behind him intellectually and to redefine himself without working through the grief.

In a delayed grief reaction that emerges into real depression, many people are simply unable to look at losses and acknowledge them. In psychological parlance, they *deny* them. For example, a divorced woman who prided herself on being beyond the guilt, hurt, and jealousy involved in the dissolution of her marriage maintained that she and her husband parted good friends. Denial is a defense used by hurt people against the pain of loss by refusing to acknowledge its existence. In "rising above" the hurt, they deny having been hurt, and so refuse to mourn their loss—until much later.

A great many people are taught to deny their grief. They are not allowed or encouraged to go through the valley of their "little deaths," all of which presage the major threat, their own death. As a result, they often carry unfinished business into their present lives and relationships.

Unresolved grief over earlier losses has been discovered to be a cause of marital conflict and unrealistic expectations of one's mate. And the courage to grieve these losses with the mate present in therapy has frequently produced a closeness that heals and reconciles the warring couple.[3] For example, in conjoint marital counseling, a man was encouraged to mourn the loss of his previous wife, to express what she had meant to him, and to say goodbye to her. His present wife was deeply moved by his tears. Subsequently, her husband ceased comparing her unconsciously with his former wife, and their conflict subsided.

The grieving person often runs into a conspiracy to keep him from going through the full course of shock, sadness, anger, and so on that are part of the grief cycle. Chaplain Robert Reeves of Columbia Presbyterian Hospital tells of a young man who had his leg amputated and went through the whole process of diagnosis, surgery, and most of the recovery period without a complaint. Admired by all during this time for his cheerfulness and bravery, he suddenly became withdrawn and depressed. His family and the hospital's medical staff became alarmed and even angry. They tried to give him pep talks to snap him out of the despondency. They failed to see that because he could not grieve, he had no alternative but to internalize the hurt in depression.[4] This fact our culture and churches still fail to grasp.

Grief reactions which are delayed or denied are usually triggered later in overreactions to smaller symbolic losses. My father died when I was nine years old, and I was encouraged—almost required—to exercise self-control at the time of his death and funeral. I was urged to "be the man of the house" and take responsibility for my mother and sister. I was not helped to mourn at the funeral or later. The presiding pastor himself was a man who seldom dealt with feelings and whose conversations were always formal. The chronic grief and persistent mourning of my widowed mother (over a period of ten years) became so repugnant to me that I could not face my own feelings of hurt and anger. In later life, I was thrown into depression by small defeats (which symbolized the "big defeat" of my father's abandonment). I often found myself despondent without any cause I could put my finger on. There came a period in my teaching career when I felt emotionally dead, bored with my classes and students, and angry with or remote from my colleagues. My pervasive mood was sadness. Ironically, it was another death that provided a new beginning. It was years later, when my beloved dog died, that I was able to release much of my pent-up sadness and anger. This crucial event activated images in my dreams which, in subsequent Jungian psychotherapy, became an important way back to emotional aliveness and a new hope.

Where the church has failed to understand the importance of mourning, psychiatry in the persons of Eric Lindemann, Gerald Caplan, and C. Murray Parkes stepped in in the 1940s and 1950s to bring us profound studies of loss, change, and grief, from which we are still learning. All have said that clergy have a central place in helping people through the grieving process during the funeral and well beyond it. Most ministers now have at least a reading knowledge of the stages of grief through which the average person passes during bereavement (see the reading list).

Easing the Expression of Anger

In delayed grief, deadness of emotion must give way to experienced feeling. A residue of anger often needs to be expressed. Foreign as that seems to the church's ethos of bland pleasantness, mature pastors and people can permit the expression of real anger. Chaplain Reeves comments:

> The person who cannot grieve but can only become angry or depressed instead, above all needs someone who will listen as he pours out the bitterest of his feelings, who will let him say the most hateful things about himself or God, without feeling compelled either to make excuses for the bereaved or to defend the good name of the Lord. Too many people, including clergymen, find this intolerable, and so they try to talk the bereaved out of his feelings, clamp down on him the platitudes of piety, smother his anger, or cheer away his guilt. Often they succeed and the anger or the guilt, apparently dispelled, is instead turned inward where it works havoc that may last for years, and sometimes even for a life-

time. . . . The only way to help him is to *listen him out*, and by accepting and trying to understand his feelings encourage him to
expel them until quietness comes. Then, and then only, is it appropriate to help his assimilate his loss . . . and begin to explore with
him how it fits into his faith. . . . It is no mark of faith to stifle grief,
but the highest faith permits a person to fling the bitterest accusa-
tions against himself or God without reproach in the certainty that
even this the Lord will accept and understand [p. 370].

Often such a necessary expression of anger is not spontaneous but needs the gentle encouragement of the pastor. It is important that anger toward self, God, family, friends, and physician be verbalized if it is present. However, the pastor should
be careful that, by encouraging anger, he does not add to the
excessive burden of guilt that most depressed people carry. I
have found three ways to "legitimize" the feelings of anger of
the inhibited parishioner. One is to demonstrate to the religious person that anger can be expressed openly and honestly
to God. The Psalms above all demonstrate this and, when appropriate, parts of relevant Psalms (for example, Psalms 43,
109, or 137) can be read to the person having trouble recognizing his feelings.

In his book on praying with the Psalmists, Thomas Troeger
makes the case that "exactly how I feel" is the starting point of
the Psalmist's (and our) prayer:

If I am awed by the majesty of God, then . . . sacred words are the
natural and fitting expression of everything I feel: "Holy, holy,
holy is the Lord of hosts; the whole earth is full of his glory." But
if I am angry that my associate has gotten a promotion because he
played up to the boss and claimed credit for ideas which were
mine, I shall pray as the psalmist did: "Vindicate me, O God, and
defend my cause . . . ; from deceitful and unjust men deliver me!"
(Psalm 43:1).[5]

Secondly, where anger is very close to the surface, I have in
some cases closed a conference with a prayer including an ar-
ticulation of the feelings I have heard: "Just when everything
was going so well for Jim, O God, we wonder why he has lost
his ability to run. It feels like you have taken his very life away,

and he is puzzled and angry. But we pray that you will help him find new life and hope that seem so distant now. . . ."

Third, where it is difficult for the person to express the anger that is revealed through his body language, I use the approach which has been called *mediate catharsis,* wherein the depressed person, once again, is not expected to express his full anger himself, but rather has it expressed for him by the pastor in words like, "If I were caught in your situation, I would be very angry." This expression by the pastor, a respected person who symbolizes faith and hope, makes the anger more acceptable and paves the way for honest acknowledgment of understandable feelings of hostility. That anger can be expressed openly (rather than through "passive aggression") by dedicated Christian people comes to many as good news (see Ephesians 4:26; Mark 3:5; Matthew 23:23–28, and John 2:13–17).

The strategies for pastoral care described above find their model in the prophetic ministry of Jeremiah. This great prophet had to awaken the grief of the people who had been numbered by the false reassurance of a monarchy which would not face the reality of impending destruction and exile. In chapters 8 to 10, Jeremiah provides a rich series of images and metaphors designed to bring grief to consciousness and uses the language of anger, grief, and lamentation to do so.

The refusal to mourn is the refusal to say goodbye to beloved persons, places, missed opportunities, vitality, or whatever has been "taken away," which is how many religious people view these losses. The refusal to mourn our earlier disappointments condemns us to live in their shadows. The inability to say goodbye may paralyze us and rigidify us, as it did Lot's wife. Genuine grief is the deep sadness and weeping that express the acceptance of our inability to do anything about our losses. It is a prelude to letting go, to relinquishment. It is a dying that precedes resurrection. Our sadness reveals what we have been invested in; it is the cost of a commitment which has been shattered.

The inability to grieve can be conceived as a form of fear—what the letter to the Hebrews (10:38) calls the urge to "shrink back" instead of meeting an unknown with faith in the God of the open future. It is a virtual denial of the God who "makes all things new."

Changing Internal Conversations

What a person says to himself about his losses or disappointments may greatly influence whether he sinks into a depressive mood or is able to reinvest his energy in new directions, goals, and relationships, in spite of defeats. It is the person's *interpretation* of events—what he tells himself about what happened—that determines his response to them.

George Hoffman (whom we met in Chapter 5) was distressed that his son, Alan, had left medical school. He blamed himself for not being a good enough father to influence his son's values. Here is an excerpt from his second session with the pastor:

GEORGE: If I had only been closer to him while I had the chance . . .

PASTOR: You seem to be saying to yourself that if you'd been an effective father, your son wouldn't have dropped out of medical school.

GEORGE: Well . . . yes . . . I guess I have been thinking that. But he's not really a puppet on my string . . .

PASTOR: Well, that's how you explain it to yourself now. But are there any other reasons why your son might have made the decision he did? Any other way you could understand what has happened?

GEORGE: Maybe the drug culture at the school got a grip on him . . . But I don't think Alan could be led around like a sheep. We've raised him to be an independent thinker . . . Guess I really don't understand his thinking . . . We were so proud of his achievements.

PASTOR: You've really wanted him to be independent, and yet it is a shock when he chooses to live in a way that is different from the way you would have chosen. Sounds like you've succeeded in teaching him independence. A very wise woman once gave me her child-rearing philosophy in two sentences: "Give your child roots. Then give him wings."

GEORGE: Maybe we've done that . . . (*long pause*). I wish I had the freedom and guts to change *my* course of life, but I'm stuck.

PASTOR: Are you? Let's look at that a bit.

The pastor has attempted to help George track his internal conversations and to look at other equally plausible explanations for Alan's decision. In the course of this exploration, his self-esteem is raised considerably.

Psychiatrist Aaron Beck[6] has successfully helped many depressed people to review their automatic thoughts and beliefs that preceded the sad mood and to correct the thoughts by answering each negative statement. He suggests the double-column technique, in which a person writes down his negative thoughts in one column and his answers opposite these. (Example: Alan has left medical school and this shows I'm a lousy father. Answer: I've tried to help him become independent. Maybe I've succeeded, but I still don't understand him.)

The journal method of written inner dialogues with oneself is another approach most pastors and parishioners can learn. It can take the form of conversational prayer, a way of articulating one's thoughts in the presence of God and seeing them in a new perspective.

Enlarging Hope

In this strategy, the pastor is basically a transition guide, helping the person to relinquish many old loves and goals and hopes and move on to the next step in his development. Enlarging hope may, paradoxically, call for lowered aspirations; hopeless projects are those which no longer fit one's circumstances.

One young college man, aspiring all of his early life to become a football linebacker, crushed several vertebrae in his first freshman football scrimmage. His hopes were shattered too. Would he give up and commit suicide, as he threatened to do? Would he become a muscular mass of indirection and bitterness, saying to himself and the world, "I must have this or nothing"? Many of his friends wondered. Agonizingly, in anger and despair, and through extended pastoral counseling, he was able to discover and affirm his early experiences of teaching handicapped children and to choose a future which included his overlooked gift. Hope, based on real potential and experienced beginnings, broke his desperate grip on goals he had clung to and encouraged him to enter unknown territory.

The loss of bodily functions, and the way of life they made possible, is a brutal blow to one's self-esteem. When hospital patients who have experienced surgery after an accident wake up to find themselves without an arm or an eye, they are often paralyzed with shock. If only they could cry or curse! And they may, later, given the proper encouragement to grieve. But despondency may come when they realize how thoroughly their lives will change. To be able to be somewhat independent and mobile again may require enormous courage, energy, and resourcefulness.

In the church, handicapped people can frequently be of great encouragement and support in those efforts. They are a hope to the depressed; they are learning to live with their handicap. One western church has created a "grief bank," a file of people who have suffered different kinds of losses in their lives who are available to counsel others. Support groups in the church help the depressed complete their grief work and get on with their lives. They befriend those going through loss and help them to know about the reactions they can expect to experience. Mutual help groups exist for almost every kind of disability: parent groups for parents who have lost a child, children's groups for those who have lost a parent or sibling, groups formed around a particular kind of illness or operation (heart disease, blindness, leukemia, mastectomy, amputation, etc.) Occasionally, the entire family or friendship network of the "patient" is included in the group. In some communities, a trained grief counselor can be enlisted to lead such group discussions. The patient's ability to maintain and broaden hope in the face of adversity is often encouraged by this supportive relationship. New skills and a new meaning for life are not acquired easily. Hope mobilizes new avenues of usefulness when helpers can imagine *with* the depressed person about his future life.

When losses are massive or irretrievable, the need for new goals and hopes is pressed relentlessly upon the person. But what if less traumatic experience has convinced a person that earlier dreams cannot be realized? In midlife, people need moral courage to enlarge their hope and to relinquish unrealistic dreams and aspirations modeled after important mentors. They need to rethink their ideas of success.

It is indispensable to the enlargement of hope that the person *review his past good experiences and accomplishments*, but not be judged by cultural success standards. It is important for depressed people to rediscover gifts they may have overlooked; to consider that roads not taken earlier may be taken now. In transitional depression, important sources of pleasure and renewal which have been pushed aside by the pressure of work and child rearing must now be reclaimed or the person dies spiritually and emotionally.

The enlargement of hope is even possible in the situation of the fatally ill person, but we must ask, "Hope for what?" For long-range survival, no. For an end to agony, perhaps. For a richer life now, yes. For a life after death? Christians are confident of that. Hope, even in terminal illness, can be enlarged. Despite the medical prognosis, the pastor's task is to help the person *live fully and creatively whatever time he has left*. People can become total invalids long before it is physically necessary. They can become bitter and make other lives miserable by their demandingness. Or they can choose to complete their lives with dignity and care for those around them. In the last days, it is hope for *being*, not primarily for *doing*, which is paramount. Every encounter is a gift for renewal. Helping people come to this realization is an expression of *sustaining* ministry.

For some people, the shock of impending death does its own

work, and they reevaluate their values as in a conversion. Humanistic psychologist Abraham Maslow spoke of his "post-mortem life" after a heart attack:

> One very important aspect of the post-mortem life is that everything gets doubly precious, gets piercingly important. You get stabbed by things, by flowers and by babies and by beautiful things—just the act of living, of walking, of breathing and eating and having friends chatting. . . . I am living an end-life where everything ought to be an end in itself, where I shouldn't waste any time preparing for the future.[7]

The end-time activates the imagination and may bring new meaning to a life.

Yet, the fatally ill patient may find his hope enlarged as he looks beyond this life into "mystery," as Thomas Wolfe did:

> To lose the earth you know, for greater knowing; to lose the life you have for greater life; to leave the friends you loved, for greater loving; to find a land more kind than home, more large than earth . . . whereon the pillars of this earth are founded, towards which the consciousness of the world is tending—a wind rising, and the rivers flow.[8]

Depression paralyzes because it is stuck in the goals and visions of the past. Hope mobilizes because it imagines a new future built on past and present reality. The model for the pastor as a transition guide in times of radical reevaluation of one's life comes through Second Isaiah, the prophet of hope, who spoke to the Hebrew exiles agonizing over their grievous dislocation and the loss of the old life:

> Remember not the former things,
>> nor consider the things of old.
> Behold, I am doing a new thing;
>> now it springs forth; do you not perceive it?
>
> (Isaiah 43:18–19, RSV)

7. Nurturing Hope in the Church

When the pastor works directly with a depressed person, he is working in the context of a community of faith; he is not alone in his ministry. The congregation is an interlocking system of relationships. A change in any one part has an impact on every other, and each impact necessarily means further change and new influence in return. Social psychiatrist Dr. Mansell Pattison concludes that "the primary function of the minister is pastoral care of the social system of the church to the end that the church system can provide the necessary basis for being."[1] What in the congregation's life and ministry promotes hopeful being? And what fosters "unhope" in that corporate body?

Some Churches May Unintentionally Cultivate Depression

What seems to kill a hopeful, forward-moving spirit in the congregation? A view of religion which assumes that ethical and religious progress is most effectively promoted, and the perils of indifference and irresponsibility are best avoided, by holding before the eyes of parishioners a vision of perfection which will keep them perpetually guilty or ashamed of themselves. Such a religious perspective measures a person against an external, preestablished standard instead of his own unique personality and temperament.

Hospital chaplain William A. Miller[2] observes from his clinical work that, in some congregations, lives have been impaired by explicit or implicit church teachings, and by the attitudes of pious parents and peers which reflect "depressogenic" views of life, including:

- a perspective which says that if the person has fears, doubts, dejection, and nagging questions, he is without faith.
- a tendency to stifle and inhibit personal feelings (for example, anger, grief, ecstasy, or sadness) and substitute a facade of false joy and pleasantness.
- a belief that conversion brings complete transformation and that no "dark" side of personality or self-serving motivations remain. Such denial gives rise to a simplistic view of a two-valued world, divided sharply between good and evil persons.
- the tendency to run life by the "tyranny of the shoulds"— a phrase borrowed from psychiatrist Karen Horney—and a legalistic demand for behavioral conformity and perfection which results in a constant state of guilt or self-deception.
- a stress on the sin and worthlessness of the unconverted human being with a tendency to see personal desires and an affirmation of one's strengths as bad; a view which believes that the more God is active in a person's life, the less

the self is active, and vice versa (a view which theologian Jonathan Edwards decisively rejects as the "see-saw" principle).

- the perspective that so stresses the identification of Jesus Christ with God that his identification with human life (with its feelings, frustrations, and temptations) is ignored. This position was the docetic heresy of earlier Christian history, and it contributes to an inability to accept truly human reactions as a part of Christian life.

Countering Despondency in the Leadership

There can be no sense of community in a congregation without a leadership that plays many roles and functions. The leadership evokes and cultivates the gifts of members of the community, with them projecting realistic goals, activating the intentionality of the group, learning to overcome frustration and powerlessness, and symbolizing the "new being" in Jesus Christ. It is crucial, therefore, that pastors and lay leaders find ways of overcoming despondency and hopelessness in their own lives.

The "causal factors" of Chapter 2 apply to any pastor's own life and ministry. In addition, occupational sources of depression in the ministry can be pinpointed. One of the most obvious causes of despondency in the pastor is the failure to mourn leaving a former church and community where bonds of friendship and trust had been established. With the inevitable sadness and anger, there is often a yearning for former ties during the first year in the new setting. Similarly, congregations must learn to mourn the loss of their former leader and his family. Such a loss cuts more deeply than people might imagine.

Ministers and lay leaders who are most disposed or vulnerable to despondency tend to be persons of very high aspirations, who are conscientious, careful in the control of their emotions, and compulsively attentive to detail. Yale University psychologist James Dittes's description of the clergyperson who has grown up as a "little adult" is pertinent here.[3] From early on, such a person has been more comfortable than most people in a care-giving, self-denying, emotionally controlled, playless role, seeking the constant approval of significant adults in his life. The person is a prime candidate for despondency.

In the parish, these ministers are strongly motivated to succeed in whatever they do. Often they are perfectionists and do not seek enjoyment or pleasure from their work but aim unconsciously at recognition or approval from those they serve, especially those in high status positions. Such a desire for approval is found in everyone, but these ministers become dejected when they do not gain it. After a few years, when they feel people are taking them for granted and simply expect them to do a good job, they become dissatisfied with themselves and their role in the church. They yearn for acceptance, not because of their performance or accomplishments, but for its own sake. Theoretically, this grace (what Paul Tillich calls acceptance) is a part of their theology, but it is not realized in their experience. They become tired and despondent. If they cannot find such affirmation in a marriage partner or friends, or if their exaggerated hopes for relationships fail to materialize, loneliness becomes another possible source of despondency.

If a leader in the church, lay or ordained, finds his life full of blandness and boredom, punctuated by periods of depression, it is likely that he is experiencing one or more of the seven crises that veteran career counselor, Thomas Brown has identified as the crucial stress points of the ministry:

- The crisis of *integrity:* feelings of fraudulence between one's real beliefs and one's profession.
- The crisis of *power:* the feeling that one lacks the power to influence a situation or people, or that the church is powerless in the world.
- The crisis of *capacity:* the feeling that one cannot do what one must do or is expected to do.
- The crisis of *failure:* the fear of failing to reach an important goal, or of failing to fulfill one's calling.

- The crisis of *destination:* a sense of the ambiguity of personal goals or church goals.
- The crisis of *role:* a conflict between self-expectations, desires, and style in leadership in the church and the expectations of the congregation.
- The crisis of *meaning:* What does it all add up to? Does it really make sense any more for me? Is this really what I am meant to be?

Clergyman-psychiatrist Paul Morentz, after counseling with a large number of pastors, describes what he calls the "frustration syndrome," which often accompanies these crises:

- The person experiences pervasive feelings of inadequacy in relationship to his work or personal relationships.
- He reacts with anger, at himself or at whatever is perceived to be the source of his frustration. He may repress an awareness of this anger, but everyone around him is aware of his irritability.
- He responds to the frustration in one of two ways: He becomes apathetic and unmotivated to do anything; or he becomes compulsively overactive, indiscriminately taking on much more than he can handle, to avoid a feeling of emptiness and guilt. He may vacillate from one mode to the other, but both seem to be void of purposive striving.

There are several avenues out of this "dark night," this discouragement-despondency cycle, that might be taken by pastors and other leaders of the church.

1. *Share your frustration and anger* with a trusted friend, a collegial group, or a professional guide.

2. *Monitor your internal conversations* about your situation. What are you saying to yourself about this event, this disappointment, or the results of your ministry? A person who has learned to track his thoughts, what he is saying to himself about his frustrating circumstances, can often get new perspective and alternate interpretations of what is happening.

3. *Encounter yourself* in the depression long enough to learn what it is trying to tell you. Don't try to do something immedi-

ately; make no important decisions until the problem is clari-
fied. It is essential to stay quiet and "engage" the despondency
before going off in a new direction with life. The use of Carl
Jung's method of "active imagination,"[4] in which one dialogues with the depression, or images of it, and with one's fantasies and daydreams, is often very helpful for finding the
message to us. It is also useful as a pastoral tool to teach others
to live with their despair long enough to find release.

4. *Evaluate your hopes and goals* (the frustration of which is being felt as discouragement) against the reasonable expectations
of this situation and your talents as a person. Often a Church
Career Development Center[5] is the best resource for increasing
the self-knowledge of pastors and their spouses. If you lack
the opportunity to participate in career assessment, workbooks
are available to help you to identify your strengths and modify
your goals (see the reading list). Involvement in continuing
education may provide fresh perspectives and the discovery of
what excites you at this stage of your life. Finding a new pas-
sion is hope-evoking and energizing.

5. *Face your fears honestly.* Are you afraid of changing your
habitual lifestyle? Of being more spontaneous and autono-
mous? Are the guaranteed status of the ministry, the provision
of housing and pension, and the need for approval standing in
the way of relinquishing your overdependence and passivity?
Parish consultant John C. Harris summarizes his research on
the fears of the pastor and congregations thus:

> To sum up, a pastor is virtually powerless to comfort or challenge
> . . . *if he is convinced he cannot survive outside the Church,* if he believes
> he cannot find work when he is ready, and if he feels he cannot
> change or influence the shape of his daily work [emphasis added].[6]

6. *Develop the "courage of imperfection"* (a phrase coined by
psychologist Alfred Adler) through meditation on God's gra-
cious love and forgiveness. Perfectionism perpetuates pretend-
ing and keeping people at a distance. A rigid self-demand for
perfection is a predisposition to depression. Of course, there
are always a few dependent, insecure parishioners who are
drawn to powerful leaders and who want a pastor who will

conceal his own neediness from them. But, as William James said, to give up pretenses is as blessed a relief as to have them gratified.

The pastor does not have to deny his pains, his hurts, and his dejection. If he goes through the wilderness creatively, those very wounds are transformed from expressions of despair into signs of hope in his ministry. Humor can help him through some of the rough times when he begins to take himself too seriously and feels that the Kingdom of God depends completely on him. As a tonic guaranteed to lift the too-heavy pastoral heart, I would prescribe for every pastor Daniel Zeluff's delightful little book, *There's Algae in the Baptismal Fount.* It will help them shed the egocentric attitudes that pastors can fall into, demonstrated in one of Zeluff's essays, "I must be a prophet, else why are they stoning me?" The writer of Proverbs was right when he said, "A cheerful heart is good medicine, but a downcast spirit dries up the bones" (Proverbs 17:22, RSV).

Telling Stories—A Road to Hopefulness

Church historian Martin Marty speaks of the "coring" functions of the church, which must be combined with its "caring" role. One of the core functions of any community of faith is to tell its stories, and to help persons to link their stories with larger, hope-evoking stories. Depressed persons need a renewed sense of meaning, and the great biblical stories can give them clues to that meaning. Psychotherapist Sheldon Kopp uses stories and metaphors as a way to show patients the universality of their suffering and to dilute their neurotic need to be special. He says to his patients, "Let me tell you a tale to ease your task."[7] The pastor or the rabbi can say, "Let me tell you a story which may help you find meaning, or good news, for your personal despondency."

The vehicles for story telling in the church can be as varied as preaching, conversations, sharing groups, liturgy, or classroom teaching.

What is significant in this post rationalistic age is that we are discovering once again to look to story and drama more than to creed and precise formulations as a way to make sense out of our suffering. Elie Weisel, a noted survivor of the Holocaust, writes all of his stories to try to make sense of that horrible event and the seemingly perennial sufferings of the Jews. He is an artist at retelling the biblical stories with this horrendous event in the background.[8]

Every discouraged person seeks the answer to Aldous Huxley's deceptively simple question, "What are people for?" As people ask what their lives are all about, they are often fed abstract ideas, precise creeds, or a ballet of bloodless concepts (too often the church's stock in trade) which seldom reach the soul with the power of an answer. There is a growing awareness that the drama, the symbols, and the stories of the church speak more deeply to the search for meaning. In Jesus's parables, the hearer's structure of expectations is attacked. Winners become losers, and vice versa. Parables have elements familiar to our own stories and an unfamiliarity that stretches and jars us. They *force us into an internal conversation about our stories that may shake the foundations.*

We need a new emphasis today on the telling of our personal stories within our religious communities; it amounts to a new way of defining personality and the work of pastoral theology. We all try to make sense of our lives by telling a story, a story that links events and our actions over time. Why am I, I and no one else? What is the inner story that I am living out? To be sure, my story is not always integrated; it doesn't always seem to be going in a single coherent direction. Often in low moods, my story is more like being lost, wandering in a desert wilderness, not knowing my way home, and feeling depressed about it; and I ask, "Why are you cast down, O my soul?"

There may be many subplots to my life, occasional detours. Sometimes a battle rages between the stories I try to tell myself: the story of a minister-professor, or of a father, or of a husband, or of a white male Christian in a world of affluence and bitter hunger. My stories may clash with those that others tell me of their existence. Warring characters are found in my

story as well: ambition and gentleness; service and self-asser-
tion; constructiveness and destructiveness; masculinity and
femininity. As I try to get the outlines straight, I also ask how
God, as coauthor of my life story, has impinged upon it; and
where chance, my own decision, and other people have played
a part. It is difficult business finding one's own story, but I am
convinced it is a human imperative for health and salvation.

Story telling, as a way of activating hope in a congregation,
involves three distinct tasks. First, parishioners (and pastors)
must be helped to discern their own unique stories. Second,
personal stories must be seen in relationship to the larger
stories of the people of God. Third, people (especially depressed people) need to be helped to rewrite and retell their
stories in the light of that confrontation.

Learning to discern the outlines of our own story is a continuous, lifelong task. Too often we settle for living the stories,
roles, and expectations that others have pushed us into, and
our own song remains unsung. The society and class and race
and gender into which we were born project their images of
the desirable self and its fulfillment as soon as we are in the
cradle. The sea of influence around us is peopled by parents,
neighbors, companions, mentors, heroes of fiction or film, all
pushing their own stories on us. How sad it is to find men and
women in midlife still trying desperately to be the boy or girl
their parents wanted them to be. People want us to meet their
expectations and so be predictable to them. And we buy into
their story and let our own shrivel up. We learn to live for the
"dominant other," a crucial characteristic of the depressed person.

In the film *I Never Sang for My Father*, it is said, "Death ends
a life, but not a relationship, which struggles on in the mind
of the survivor toward some resolution." Such a dependent tie
may exist even after death.

Kierkegaard was well aware that the deepest cause of despair was the unwillingness to be one's unique, finite self. He
wrote:

When the ambitious man whose watchword is "either Caesar or

nothing" does not become Caesar, he is in despair. . . . But this signifies something else, namely, that precisely because he did not become Caesar, he cannot endure to be himself.[9]

Attempting to live a life that does not fit is a prime cause of
depression. Jung believed that one cannot get rid of one's self
in favor of an artificial personality without repercussions in
the form of fears, irritability, and depressive moods. Depression and boredom may be signals that we must find our own
personal myth (story) to live by. Individuation is an inward
necessity, especially after age forty, and it may be God's way of
nudging us, calling us toward our authentic story and rediscov-
very of our smoldering capacities for life which are buried under our depression. The church can minister to its people by
prompting them to ask: "Have I discovered the story most appropriate to my potentialities? Are there elements of my
uniqueness in it? Is it addressed to the times in which we live
and what needs to be done in the world? Where is it in har-
mony, and where in tension, with the stories of those I live
with in community?"

The second task is to help a congregation respond to the
larger stories in order to find an umbrella for their personal
stories. This does not mean they will always respond positive-
ly. We resonate with certain TV shows or movies that grasp us.
We are gripped by some fairy tales and myths. The stories we
respond to both reflect and challenge our stories. Just so, the
special character of the biblical stories is that they are told not
for themselves alone; they are always about us. They locate us
in the midst of the larger story of God's people and relate us to
the great dramatist and storyteller, God. They are stories that
read us.

Christian nurture is to help me recognize myself in the
events of the biblical story: in the painful trek of the Exodus
and the eagerness to turn back to the safety of my predictable
Egypt; in Jacob's wrestling with God all night on the verge of
a major transition in his life; in the garden hiding from God,
myself, and those I love, as God asks, "Where are you, Adam
(man-woman), after all these years of this kind of duplicity?" I
can begin to see the meaning of death and resurrection as I re-

flect on the ego-wounds and discouragements of my life and understand that real growth would never have occurred without those hurts. I begin to understand how, through Christ's suffering and dying, victory can come. I can feel one with Nicodemus as he brings his middle-aged self (with its sense of "stuckness" and shattered dreams) to Jesus in the middle of the night, asking how to find a new quality of life that is eternal. I am with him when he wonders, after Jesus's answer, how he can be born anew when all the grooves of his life have been dug so deeply into depressive routines. The Bible's story shocks me into awareness because it is my self-portrayal; it may speak to me more deeply than any story I've confronted, and I may be led to say, "That's my story too."

More usually, I may find some tension between the church's story of faith and the other stories I confront in my life. Theologian Robert McAfee Brown describes the conflict:

> I am constantly balancing—or juggling—a number of ways of telling my own story: the masculine version, the American version, the human version, the Christian version, the university professor version, and so on. But I am also constantly reviewing those stories of my time: the feminine version, the Black version, the Third World version, the Jewish version, the Buddhist version. . . . Within this multitude of stories, I accord one story, or several stories, a higher authority than others. . . . If things go well, my normative story is authenticated. . . . But things may not go well. My normative story may be so badly challenged or shattered that I must painfully reconstruct a new story for myself.[10]

The congregation which intends to become an agent of hope will help people to explore honestly the dominant myths of their lives and to make a judgment about them. At the same time, it presents the gospel story as intimately related to their stories. "The chief vocation of the minister is to continuously make connections between the human story and the divine story," says Henri Nouwen, who describes the pastor as "the healing reminder," "the sustaining reminder," and "the guiding reminder."[11]

The third crucial task is to help people retell their stories in a new way in light of the biblical understanding of life. This is a lifelong, dynamic process. As a spiritual director, the minister is engaged in a continuous process of formation and guidance, in which the Christian is led and encouraged in his special calling. As a "living reminder," the pastor also helps people find ultimate meaning and hope in the face of the polarities of their lives.

Life is the story of conflict, and will continue to be so. Indeed, it is the tension of opposing needs that gives life its energy and vitality. The polarities of existence are basic to us as human beings. This biblical view of life reflects Buddhist and early Greek thought as well. Each pole must be recognized and affirmed to keep life vital and, ultimately, hopeful. To grant a place in our lives to only one of the pair, denying the opposite and its power, is to condemn that opposite to clandestine and indirect expression, and ourselves to a sense of hopelessness.

The one-sided church inadvertently fosters depression; it fails to recognize the polarities as part of religious experience. It fails to recognize a place for both grace and responsibility ("Everything I do is governed by the spirit of God"); both being and becoming ("I am saved; I have arrived"); both constructiveness and destructiveness ("I am loving, but God will condemn those who are not like me").

Our wholeness and our hope depend on finding a way to embrace and yet reconcile the polarities and paradoxes of our lives. We are free, yet bound; sinners, yet saints; aware of a destination, yet on a lifelong journey; called to deny, yet to affirm the self; under a mercy which is perfectly free, yet demanding. It is the Christian's conviction that in the cross of Christ the opposites can be held together, as can the vertical and horizontal, and that ultimately we shall be beyond conflict. Meanwhile, the tension of opposites provides the energy for life, even as the polarity of positive and negative poles is capable of producing electrical power.

Retelling one's story in light of the polarities of existence brings a realism which avoids both optimism and pessimism. Such retelling fosters hope because it does not ignore the conflicts of real life and is not surprised at life's reversals. Spiritual guides will be aware of and will honor the tensions within the maturing life: the pulls of inner and outer nature, freedom and destiny, grace and gratitude, providence and trust, young and old, destruction and creation, masculine and feminine, attachment and separateness.[12]

Without Vision, the People Perish

Human beings are incurably eschatological; that is, they need a vision of where life is heading and how their purposes fit into the picture. As Sam Keen says, to avoid despair, "human intentionality must be a moment within the intentionality of the cosmos." We cannot live in a bare succession of "nows." We find more by the pull of the future than by a push from the past. Whether that future is imagined as a technological paradise, a new Zion, the biblical Kingdom of God, *The Sane Society* of Erich Fromm, or the *Walden Two* of B.F. Skinner, some larger vision is necessary to save us from despair.

The church has long been divided on whether the ultimate expression of "thy Kingdom come" will be a contradiction or a continuity of the best we have seen in human life. Should the ultimate Christian hope be expressed in the vision of one final event which constitutes a basic reversal of all the unresolved problems of human existence? Or should Christian hope be expressed as confidence in God as a compassionate "directivity" toward what-is-not-yet but what has been experienced as a foretaste of our life together? Clearly, I take the latter position. Yet I have little confidence that abstract statements about that final outcome can generate hope in the church in anywhere near the same degree as people already living in God's future.

Such people symbolize God's hope because *they live beyond the success and failure* which so dominate our lives and contribute to our depression and our pride and ego-inflation. They have a peace which passes understanding. They seem to embody a hope that goes beyond their hopes, many of which have been dashed. Knowing who they are and Whose they are, they give an intimation of that freedom in Christ which all will someday realize.

A university professor whom I knew as a graduate student

reports his experience of one such person who had moved
from despair to hope and so was able to activate hope in others.

> I had come to Vienna after a two-week illness in a little Austrian
> village. I had spent most of my travel money on medicine and doc-
> tors and used my last bit to take a train to Vienna. I had no clue as
> to where I could find my friends who had been waiting for me ear-
> lier. I was lost and hungry and depressed. As I was standing in one
> of the streetcar stations in the center of the city, tired, discouraged,
> and trying to figure out what to do, a little, old wrinkled woman
> (whose job it was to sweep out the station) came over to me and
> asked if I was hungry. Even before I could answer, she took her
> lunch from a brown bag and offered me half. I was moved. She not
> only helped my aching hunger, but lifted my spirit in an unforget-
> table way. I have never forgotten her—the warmth of her face, the
> graciousness of her gift, the youthful sparkle in her eyes. We
> talked for more than an hour about her life. It had not been easy.
> She was raised in the country, knowing nothing but hard work on
> a farm. She had lost her husband and two sons in the Resistance.
> Only her daughter had survived. But she was thankful, she said,
> for many things. She was at peace with her story. Finally, I asked
> her why she offered me her lunch. She said simply, "Jesu ist mein
> Herr. Gott ist gut." [Jesus is my Lord. God is good.] She understood
> and lived the story of Jesus in a way that the most sophisticated
> scholars could never do. Her faith touched mine. Who was it, after
> all, that I met that day in Vienna?[13]

Notes

Chapter 1

1. Martin Buber, "Guilt and Guilt Feelings," trans. R. G. Smith. The William Alanson White Memorial Lectures, Fourth Series, *Psychiatry* (May 1957), pp. 114–29.
2. Leslie F. Brandt, *Psalms/Now* (St. Louis: Concordia, 1973), p. 23.
3. Maggie Scarf, "The More Sorrowful Sex," *Psychology Today*, April 1979, pp. 45–52, 89.
4. Martin E. P. Seligman, *Helplessness: On Depression, Development and Death* (San Francisco: W. H. Freeman, 1975).
5. Jessie Bernard, "Homosociality and Female Depression," *Journal of Social Issues*, 32 (1976), pp. 213–238.
6. Eda LeShan, *Learning to Say Goodbye (When a Parent Dies)* (New York: Macmillan, 1976).
7. Nathan Kline, *From Sad to Glad* (New York, Ballantine, 1974).

Chapter 2

1. I would recommend the following books for more detailed discussion of some of the theories referred to in this chapter: Silvano Arieti, and Jules Bemporad, *Severe and Mild Depressions: The Psychotherapeutic Approach* (New York: Basic Books, 1978); Aaron T. Beck, *Depression* (New York: Harper &

Row, 1967); Frederic Flach, *The Secret Strength of Depression* (New York: Bantam Books, 1975); Frederic Flach and Susanne Draghi (eds.), *The Nature and Treatment of Depression* (New York: Wiley, 1975); Alexander Lowen, *Depression and the Body* (Baltimore, Md.: Penguin Books, 1972).

2. Arieti and Bemporad, *Severe and Mild Depressions*, p. 54.
3. Roger Gould, *Transformations: Growth and Change in Adult Life* (New York: Simon & Schuster, 1978).
4. Elliot Jaques, "Death and the Midlife Crisis," *International Journal of Psychoanalysis* 46 (1965), pp. 502–514.
5. Anne Schaffer (ed.), *Dear Deedee* (Secaucus, N.J.: Lyle Stuart, 1978).
6. Lynn Caine, *Widow* (New York: Bantam, 1975).
7. C. G. Jung, *Psychological Reflections*, ed. Jolande Jacobi (New York: Pantheon, 1953), p. 222.
8. See, for example: Aaron T. Beck, A. John Rush, Brian F. Shaw, and Gary Emery, *Cognitive Therapy of Depression* (New York: Guilford, 1979); Albert Ellis, *Reason and Emotion in Psychotherapy* (New York: Lyle Stuart, 1962); Victor Raimey, *Misunderstandings of the Self* (San Francisco: Jossey-Bass, 1975).
9. In Beck, *Depression*, pp. 255–256.
10. Sigmund Freud, "Mourning and Melancholia" (1917), in *Collected Works*, Vol. 4, trans. Joan Riviere (New York: Basic Books, 1959), pp. 152–170.
11. William A. Miller, *Why Do Christians Break Down?* (Minneapolis: Augsburg 1973).
12. C. S. Lewis, *A Grief Observed* (New York: Bantam, 1976).
13. Robert Kemper, *An Elephant's Ballet: The Story of One Man's Struggle with Sudden Blindness* (New York: Seabury, 1977), p. 71.
14. Dennis Linn and Matthew Linn, *Healing Life's Hurts* (New York: Paulist Press, 1978).
15. Karl Menninger, *Whatever Became of Sin?* (New York: Bantam Books, 1978).
16. James G. Emerson, *The Dynamics of Forgiveness* (Philadelphia: Westminster, 1964).
17. Edward V. Stein, *Guilt: Theory and Therapy* (Philadelphia: Westminster, 1968); Paul Tournier, *Guilt and Grace* (New York: Harper & Bros., 1962); Dennis Linn and Matthew Linn, *Healing Life's Hurts* (New York: Paulist Press, 1978).
18. C. G. Jung, "Two Essays on Analytical Psychology," in *The Collected Works*, Vol. 7, 2nd ed. (Princeton, N.J.: Princeton University Press, 1966), p. 215.
19. C. G. Jung, "The Stages of Life." In *The Portable Jung*, ed. Joseph Campbell (New York: Viking, 1971).
20. June Singer, *Boundaries of the Soul* (Garden City, N.Y.: Doubleday, 1972), p. 359.
21. C. G. Jung, *Modern Man in Search of a Soul* (New York: Harcourt, Brace 1933), p. 264.
22. Nathan Kline, *From Sad to Glad* (New York: Ballantine, 1974); Ronald R. Fieve, *Moodswing* (New York: Bantam, 1976).
23. See sources listed in Note 1.
24. Beck, *Cognitive Therapy and the Emotional Disorders* (New York: International Universities Press, 1976), pp. 303–304.

25. Sam Keen, "Boredom and How to Beat It," *Psychology Today*, May 1977, p. 84.

26. Arieti and Bemporad, *Severe and Mild Depressions*, pp. 388–389.

Chapter 3

1. Seward Hiltner, *Preface to Pastoral Theology* (Nashville, Tenn.: Abingdon, 1958); and *The Christian Shepherd: Some Aspects of Pastoral Care* (Nashville, Tenn.: Abingdon, 1959).

2. William A. Clebsch and Charles R. Jaekle, *Pastoral Care in Historical Perspective* (Englewood Cliffs, N.J.: Prentice-Hall, 1964).

3. C. W. Brister, *Pastoral Care in the Church* (New York: Harper & Row, 1964).

4. Daniel Day Williams, *The Minister and the Care of Souls* (New York: Harper & Bros., 1961), p. 147.

5. The Suicide Prevention Center of Marin County, California, for example, has a grief counseling training program open to both clergy and laity designed, in part, to help bereaved people and "survivors of sudden death" counter the depression that would follow inadequate sorrow work. It involves a minimum of forty hours of supervised training. Grief counseling programs have now been inaugurated by trained pastors in a number of churches.

   A West Coast church has created a training program for lay counseling of depressed persons, taught by a pastoral counseling specialist. It is estimated that about 50 percent of the trainees are able to function very well in this specialized area of pastoral care.

6. Don S. Browning, *The Moral Context of Pastoral Care* (Philadelphia: Westminster, 1976).

7. Clebsch and Jaekle, *Pastoral Care;* and Hiltner, *Preface to Pastoral Theology.*

8. Gabriel Marcel, *Homo Viator: Introduction to a Metaphysic of Hope* (New York: Harper Torchbook, 1962).

9. William F. Lynch, *Images of Hope* (Baltimore: Helicon Press, 1965).

10. Ezra Stotland, *The Psychology of Hope* (San Francisco: Jossey-Bass, 1969).

11. Paul Tillich, *The Shaking of the Foundations* (New York: Scribner's, 1948).

12. Nikos Kazantzakis, *Zorba the Greek* (New York: Simon & Schuster, 1952), pp. 120–121.

13. Paul W. Pruyser, *The Minister as Diagnostician: Personal Problems in Pastoral Perspective* (Philadelphia: Westminster, 1976), p. 66.

14. Ira Progoff, "The Dynamics of Hope and the Image of Utopia," in *Eranos Jahr Buch* (Zurich: Rhein-Verlag, 1964), pp. 107–108.

15. Walter Brueggemann, "The Formfulness of Grief," *Interpretation,* January 1978, p. 270.

16. Carl R. Rogers, "Some Elements of Effective Interpersonal Communication." (An unpublished paper, privately circulated, 1965.)

17. Anton T. Boisen, *Out of the Depths* (New York: Harper & Bros., 1960), p. 96.

Chapter 4

1. Erik Erikson, *Childhood and Society* (New York: Norton, 1950), p. 20.
2. Cited in Henri Ellenberger, *The Discovery of the Unconscious* (New York: Basic Books, 1970), p. 44.
3. Langdon Gilkey, *Naming the Whirlwind: The Renewal of God-Language* (New York: Bobbs-Merrill, 1969), p. 240.
4. Gaylord B. Noyce, "Has Ministry's Nerve Been Cut by the Pastoral Counseling Movement?" *Christian Century*, February 1–8, 1978, p. 103.
5. Robert Bendiksen and Philip L. Berg, "Religion and Life Crisis Counseling: Perceptions of Clergy Effectiveness." A research report presented at the annual meeting of the Society for the Scientific Study of Religion, Chicago, October 28–30, 1977.
6. Walter Brueggemann, "Covenanting as Human Vocation," *Interpretation*, Vol. 33, No. 2, April 1979.
7. Paul Tillich, "The Meaning of Providence." In *The Shaking of the Foundations* (New York: Scribner's, 1948), pp. 106–107.
8. Williams, *The Minister and the Care of Souls*, p. 42.
9. Paul Pruyser, "Narcissism in Contemporary Religion," *Journal of Pastoral Care* 33 (December 1978), p. 229.
10. Paul Pruyser, "The Use and Neglect of Pastoral Resources," *Pastoral Psychology*, September 1972, p. 5.
11. Progoff, "The Dynamics of Hope," p. 94.
12. Howard Thurman, *The Mood of Christmas* (New York: Harper & Row, 1973).
13. Jerome D. Frank, *Persuasion and Healing* (New York: Schocken, 1963), p. 63.
14. Gerald Gurin, Joseph Veroff, and Sheila Field, *Americans View Their Mental Health* (New York: Basic Books, 1960).
15. Ruth B. Caplan, *Helping the Helpers to Help* (New York: Seabury, 1972).

Chapter 5

1. Karl Menninger, *Whatever Became of Sin?* p. 201.
2. Richard A. Kulka, Joseph Veroff, and Elizabeth Dowvan, "Social Class and the Use of Professional Help for Personal Problems," *Journal of Health and Social Behavior* 20 (March 1979), pp. 2–17.
3. For example, psychiatrists increased from 5,800 in 1950 to 27,000 in 1975. In California alone, licensed marriage, family, and child counselors have increased by 10,000 in the last ten years, according to the American Psychiatric Association and the California Department of Consumer Affairs.
4. Bendiksen and Berg, "Religion and Life Crisis Counseling."
5. A beginning inquiry into this important subject can be made by consulting the following (arranged according to date published): Gordon Allport, *The Individual and His Religion* (New York: Macmillan, 1950); David Roberts, *Psychotherapy and a Christian View of Man* (New York: Scribner's, 1950); Anton Boisen, *Exploration of the Inner World* (New York: Harper & Bros., 1952); James Loder, *Religious Pathology and Christian Faith* (Philadelphia: Westmin-

ster, 1966); Paul Pruyser, *A Dynamic Psychology of Religion* (New York: Harper & Row, 1968); Wayne Oates, *When Religion Gets Sick* (Philadelphia: Westminster, 1970); Merton Strommen (ed.), *Research in Religious Development*, especially chapters by Bernard Spilka, James Dittes, Russell Becker, and Roy Fairchild (New York: Hawthorn, 1970); Don Browning, *Generative Man* (Philadelphia: Westminster, 1974).

6. William Oglesby, *Referral in Pastoral Counseling* (Englewood Cliffs, N.J.: Prentice-Hall, 1968).

7. Of particular value to the pastor will be Aaron Beck's "Depression Inventory," which taps the areas of sadness, sense of failure, dissatisfaction, guilt, suicidal ideas, social withdrawal, insomnia, work retardation, etc. It is included in his book *Depression* (New York: Harper & Row, 1967) or is available from The Center for Cognitive Therapy, Room 602, 133 South 36th Street, Philadelphia, PA 19104.

8. See note 1, Chapter 2, for sources of statistics.

9. Chapter 5 of Lee Ann Hoff's excellent book *People in Crisis* (Menlo Park, Cal.: Addison-Wesley, 1978) contains some concrete suggestions for dealing with this ambivalent attitude toward living and dying.

10. Robert L. Mason, Carol B. Currier, and John R. Curtis, *The Clergyman and the Psychiatrist—When to Refer* (Chicago: Nelson-Hall, 1978).

11. Caplan, *Helping the Helpers to Help*, pp. 39–40.

12. Arieti and Bemporad, *Severe and Mild Depressions*, p. 86.

13. R. Fairchild, Orville G. Brim, and Edgar F. Borgatta "Relations Between Family Problems," in M. Sussman (ed.), *Sourcebook in Marriage and the Family*, rev. ed. (New York: Houghton-Mifflin, 1962).

14. Robert S. Weiss, *Marital Separation* (New York: Basic Books, 1975), pp. 51–52.

15. Leonard Cammer, *Up from Depression* (New York: Pocket Books, 1969).

Chapter 6

1. From T. H. Holmes and R. H. Rahe, "The Social Adjustment Rating Scales," *Journal of Psychosomatic Research* 11 (1967), pp. 213–218. Copyright 1967, Pergamon Press, Ltd. Reprinted by permission.

2. Colin Murray Parkes, *Bereavement: Studies of Grief in Adult Life* (New York: International Universities Press, 1972), p. 7.

3. Norman Paul, "The Role of Mourning and Empathy in Conjoint Marital Therapy," in G. H. Zuk and I. Boszormenyi-Nagy (eds.), *Family Therapy and Disturbed Families* (Palo Alto, Calif.: Science and Behavior Books, 1967).

4. Robert B. Reeves, Jr., "The Hospital Chaplain Looks at Grief," in Bernard Schoenberg, Arthur C. Carr, David Peretz, and Austin Kutscher (eds.), *Loss and Grief: Psychological Management in Medical Practice* (New York: Columbia University Press, 1970), p. 362.

5. Thomas Troeger, *Rage! Reflect. Rejoice!: Praying with the Psalmists* (Philadelphia: Westminster, 1977), p. 13.

6. Aaron Beck and Ruth Greenberg, *Coping with Depression* (New York: Institute for Rational Living, 1974).

7. Abraham Maslow, in *Psychology Today*, August 1970, p. 16.
8. Thomas Wolfe, *You Can't Go Home Again* (New York: Harper & Row, 1940), p. 743.

Chapter 7

1. Mansell Pattison, *Pastor and Parish: A Systems Approach* (Philadelphia: Fortress Press, 1977), p. 12.
2. William A. Miller, *Why Do Christians Break Down?* (Minneapolis: Augsburg, 1973), pp. 30–32.
3. Strommen, *Research and Religions Development*, Ch. 11.
4. See C. G. Jung, *Collected Works*, Vol. 14 (Princeton: Princeton University Press, 1974), pp. 495–496; Marie-Louise Von Franz, *C. G. Jung: His Myth in Our Time* (New York: C. G. Jung Foundation and Putnam's, 1975); and Ann Ulanov and Barry Ulanov, *Religion and the Unconscious* (Philadelphia: Westminster, 1975).
5. Write the Church Career Development Council, 66 East 15th Avenue, Columbus, OH 43201.
6. John C. Harris, *Stress, Power, and Ministry* (Washington, D.C.: The Alban Institute, 1977), p. 165.
7. Sheldon Kopp, *The Hanged Man* (Palo Alto, Calif.: Science and Behavior Books, 1974) Also see Kopp's other books on the therapy of story or metaphor: *Guru* (1971); *If You Meet the Buddha on the Road, Kill Him* (1972), and *This Side of Tragedy*, (1977) by the same publisher.
8. See especially his *Messengers of God: Biblical Portraits and Legends* (New York: Random House, 1976).
9. Søren Kierkegaard, *Fear and Trembling and The Sickness Unto Death* (Garden City, N.Y.: Doubleday Anchor, 1954).
10. Robert McAfee Brown, "My Story and the Story," *Theology Today*, July 1975, p. 167.
11. Henri Nouwen, *The Living Reminder* (New York: Seabury, 1977), p. 24.
12. For penetrating observations on the importance of polarities, see Seward Hiltner, *Theologicai Dynamics* (Nashville, Tenn.: Abingdon, 1972). Daniel Levinson (with Charlotte N. Darrow, Edward B. Klein, Maria H. Levinson, and Braxton McKee), extending the ideas of C. G. Jung, see confrontation with the great polarities as the chief task of midlife individuation in *The Seasons of a Man's Life* (New York: Knopf, 1978).
13. From personal correspondence with Craig Schindler.

For Further Reading

Certain topics alluded to in the text, though related to depression and hope, could not be discussed in full. The following references will help the reader to pursue these subjects in more detail.

Grief and Bereavement

Jackson, Edgar. *The Many Faces of Grief*. Nashville, Tenn.: Abingdon, 1977.

Kübler-Ross, Elizabeth. *On Death and Dying*. New York: Macmillan, 1969.

LeShan, Eda. *Learning to Say Good-by: When a Parent Dies*. New York: Macmillan, 1976.

Lewis, C.S. *A Grief Observed*. New York: Bantam Books, 1976.

Oates, Wayne E. *Pastoral Care and Counseling in Grief and Separation*. Philadelphia: Fortress, 1976.

Schoenberg, Bernard; Carr, Arthur C.; Peretz, David; and Kutscher, Austin H., eds. *Loss and Grief: Psychological Management in Medical Practice*. New York: Columbia University Press, 1970.

Spiegel, Yorick. *The Grief Process: Analysis and Counseling*. Translated by Elsbeth Duke. Nashville, Tenn.: Abingdon, 1977.

Temes, Roberta. *Living with an Empty Chair—A Guide Through Grief.* Amherst, Mass.: Mandala, 1977.

Suicide Prevention and Crisis Intervention

Hatton, Laura; Valente, Sharon; and Alice Rink, eds. *Suicide: Assessment and Intervention.* New York: Appleton-Century-Crofts, 1977.

Hoff, Lee Ann. *People in Crisis: Understanding and Helping.* Menlo Park, Cal.: Addison-Wesley, 1978.

Klagsbrun, Francine. *Youth and Suicide.* New York: Pocket Books, 1977.

Pretzel, Paul W. *Understanding and Counseling the Suicidal Person.* Nashville, Tenn.: Abingdon, 1972.

Stone, Howard. *Crisis Counseling.* Philadelphia: Fortress, 1976.

Transitional Depression in Midlife

Gould, Roger. *Transformations: Growth and Change in Adult Life.* New York: Simon and Schuster, 1978.

Keen, Sam. *Beginnings Without End.* New York: Harper & Row, 1975.

Levinson, Daniel J. (with Darrow, Charlotte N.; Klein, Edward B.; Levinson, Maria H.; and McKee, Braxton). *The Seasons of a Man's Life.* New York: Knopf, 1978.

Mayer, Nancy. *The Male Mid-life Crisis.* New York: Doubleday, 1978.

Raines, Robert. *Going Home.* New York: Harper & Row, 1979.

Life Review and Lifestory Perspectives

Butler, Robert N.; and Lewis, Myrna I. *Aging and Mental Health: Positive Psychosocial Approaches.* New York: Mosby, 1977.

Fairchild, Roy W. *Lifestory Conversations.* New York: United Presbyterian Church, 1977.

Jenkins, Sara. *Past Present: Recording Life Stories of Older People.* Washington, D.C.: National Council on Aging (1828 L. St., Washington, D.C. 20036), 1978.

Keen, Sam; and Fox, Anne Valley. *Telling Your Story.* New York: Doubleday, 1973.

Shea, John. *Stories of God: An Unauthorized Biography.* Chicago: Thomas More Press, 1978.

TeSelle, Sallie. *Speaking in Parables.* Philadelphia: Fortress, 1975.

Life Planning and Career Assessment

Bolles, Richard. *What Color is Your Parachute?—A Practical Manual for Job-hunters and Career-changers.* Berkeley, Cal.: Ten Speed Press, 1972.

Crystal, John C.; and Bolles, Richard N. *Where Do I Go From Here With My Life?* New York: Seabury, 1974.

Haldane, Bernard. *Career Satisfaction and Success: A Guide to Job Freedom.* New York: American Management Association, 1978.

Miller, Arthur; and Mattson, Ralph. *The Truth about You.* New York: Revell, 1972.

The Journal Method of Written Dialogues

Downs, Tom. *A Journey to Self Through Dialogue.* West Mystic, Conn.: Twenty-third Publications, 1977.

Progoff, Ira. *At a Journal Workshop.* New York: Dialogue House Library, 1975.

Simons, George F. *Keeping Your Personal Journal.* New York: Paulist Press, 1978.

Index